NORTH CASCADES NATIONAL PARK

Skagit River

Marblemount

Cascade River

Rockport

Illabot Creek

Sauk River

N. Fork Stillaguamish

Suiattle River

N

0   2   5   10 miles

③.The River   ④.Greater Skagit Flats   ⑤.Shorelines & Bays   ⑥.The Islands   7. Leaving a Natural Legacy

Fireweed on Sauk Mountain.

Steve Philbrick

Natural Skagit

A Journey from Mountains to Sea

SKAGIT LAND TRUST
Saving Land for Tomorrow

www.skagitlandtrust.org

TABLE OF CONTENTS

PHOTOGRAPHERS

Al Anderson • Winston Anderson • Brett Baunton • Diane Bednarz • Steve Berentson • Michelle Blaine • Pat Buller • Martin Burwash • Sandy Carter • Robert Cash • Tim Chandonnet • Kelli Christoferson • Wade Clark Jr. • Andrew Cline • Nathan Cranston • Denise Crowe • Brenda Cunningham • Benj Drummond • Jerry Eisner • Todd Entrikin • Corwin Fergus • Natalie Fobes • Suzanne Fogarty • Dick Garvey • Phil Green • Pete Haase • Jerry Haegele • Nicole Herman • Jan Hersey • Dan Hilden • Tony Jewell • Michael Kirshenbaum • Christine Kitch • Thea LaCross • Bryce Mann • Lee Mann • Tim Manns • Eddie McHugh • Erin McKay • Ric Merry • Libby Mills • Kirsten Morse • Therese Ogle • Raymond Parsons • Geoff Peterson • Steve Philbrick • Thomas Plank • Neil Rabinowitz • Jim Ramaglia • Mary Randlett • Margaret Saint Clair • Steve Satushek • Kelley Scarzafava • John Scurlock • Jan Searle • John Sedgwick • Rosemary Seifreid • Dave Smith • Dick Smith • Andrew Szurek • Kevin Thurner • Theresa Trebon • Nancy Wagner • Keith Wiggers

"The Skagit"

Throughout this book we reference the geographic region of Skagit County by several names that are used locally and interchangeably including: Skagit County, The Skagit, Skagit, and Skagit Valley.

Natural Skagit *is published by Skagit Land Trust, a non-profit organization committed to leaving a natural legacy of wildlife habitat, farms, forests, shorelines, and marine areas for current and future generations in Skagit County, Washington. This book grew out of Skagit Land Trust's collaborative approach to conservation. It began as an idea to inspire people to conserve the best of the stunningly beautiful Skagit for future generations and blossomed into a process that brought together people of varying conservation viewpoints for the common goal of creating this book.*

Project manager and graphic designer Patricia Chambers of ECANDO and Renata Hoyle Maybruck of Skagit Land Trust led the steering and photographic committees through a journey of inspiration, communication, collaboration, and hard work. We are deeply indebted to numerous people in our community who assisted with the book and to those who agreed to be interviewed. We asked people to speak from their own conservation voice, knowing that incorporating varied viewpoints is the crux of lasting conservation. In today's world, everything is connected. That is how Skagit Land Trust approached this book and how we approach land conservation. We hope this book will inspire us all to save land for tomorrow. —Molly Doran, Executive Director, Skagit Land Trust

« Photo Facing Page: Lee Mann

COVER PHOTOGRAPHS: Front Cover: Sauk Mountain View, Todd Entrikin | Front Cover, Bottom (left to right): El Dorado, Benj Drummond; Fiddle-head Fern, Steve Satushek; Tulips, Wade Clark Jr.; Bald Eagle, Lee Mann | Back Cover: Meadow Stream, Kevin Thurner • COVER DESIGN: Patricia Chambers • TITLE PAGE PHOTO: Pat Buller

They Call It the Magic Skagit.

Tom Robbins

A river runs through it, travels down the valley like a liquid train, hauling steelhead and silt, hauling snowmelt and driftwood, hauling fir needles, spilled huckleberries, the furtive shadows of ghost dancers and Sasquatch, the lost feathers of bald eagle, raven, woodpecker and loon. A river runs through it, the old primeval express, its boxcars two-thirds hydrogen, one-third oxygen; powered by the Great God Gravity, emerging unannounced from a subterranean station in the Canadian Cascades, gathering speed, whistling past the stay-at-home boulders, mocking every slowpoke glacier, running with such primal vigor that it takes three major dams to flag its energy, and even then it refuses to rest until it can taste in its mouth that sea salt for which all rivers hunger as much or more than they thirst for rain.

Thomas Plank

A river runs the length of the Skagit Valley, 160 miles all the way, and whereas upstream it runs lively and green, its musical gurgle competing mainly with ax chop, owl hoot, and the whisper of alder leaves, downstream it turns sullen and opaque, its sing-song supplanted by tractor drone. Whereas upstream, cutting through the forest with a jadite track, it offers its water to those otters, cougars and bears who bend on its gravel strands to drink, downstream it nourishes a flat expanse of farmland so fertile that should you stick your fork in the soil, juice would likely spurt.

If upstream the valley is both more rustic and pristine, the conifers thicker, the frosted pinnacles more theatrically in your face, the downstream delta boasts its own litany of charms. It's down there (where cloud-bowls of silver oyster light spill onto the tide flats, the dikes, the sloughs and the cattailed campus of the University of Mud); it's there that agriculture, art and wild nature commingle in an unprecedented mix. It's there that the Skagit spreads its broad tablecloth, setting it with cabbages, strawberries, spinach and clams; decorating it with more tulips than a bargeload of Dutch boys could count in a month. It's there and nowhere else that blue herons wade in paint jars and poets sling peas at the moon.

Speaking of Dutch boys, the valley could use a few in the long rainy season. Flooding, however, is part of a river's job description, its birthright, and that same drenching that can lead the Skagit to get too big for its britches also ensures that our streams never become too shallow to support the mystic journey of migrating salmon, our collective totem and the earth's most perfect fish. Wet weather enlivens the moss, bejewels the ferns, emboldens the gastropods (Who let the snails out?), causes mushrooms to rise like loaves, and year after year frescoes the valley with an emerald brush.

Yes, it's the Magic Skagit, so called, and a river runs through it like a fugitive freight line, hauling the sweat of struggling farmers, hauling the tears of dispossessed tribes, hauling the snoose of callous loggers, the drool of greedy developers and the slime of corrupt politicos; yet also transporting the dreams of those who work to preserve and protect this increasingly threatened swan-blanched drizzleland, the enlightened who recognize that maintaining a respect—nay, a *reverence!*—for wildness, for the Skagit's raw peaks, dark arbors and primordial bogs, is an essential component of what it means to be truly human, truly alive.

Pat Buller

Tom Robbins, internationally known for his offbeat yet popular and influential fiction, is the author of eight seriocomic novels, six of which were New York Times bestsellers. All are still in print. He has lived in the Skagit Valley since 1970.

The Skagit &
Her People

Craig Romano

Born of melting snow and ice in the far northern reaches of the Cascade Mountains and fed by a vast network of creeks, rivers, and moisture from the sky, the Skagit River careens, churns, and chugs westward for over 160 miles, emptying its life-sustaining waters into Washington's immense inland sea. Offshore, processions of dark moisture-laden clouds congregate, waiting to charge the valleys and hills and steep jagged mountains that embrace the mighty waterway and its tributaries.

Throughout the seasons, precipitation ebbs and flows. The majestic river rises and falls; its force intensifies and wanes, constantly in flux, yet always striving for balance.

For at least 10,000 years, Coast Salish tribes and their ancestors relied upon

« Lee Mann

the Skagit for its nourishing bounties. Like the land, these First Nations were also in flux striving for balance. They centered their lives in small villages along the river, its major tributaries, and the coastal flats at the head of the valley. Their relatively stable populations meant that the flourishing salmon stocks, which they depended upon for their survival, weren't depleted. The ancient towering cedars that sheltered and clothed them (and provided them mobility in the form of canoes) weren't overharvested. The Skagit ecosystem was able to replenish what was taken.

But by the late 1700s, the region's ecological balance began to tilt. From the east, a counter-force more powerful and transformative than the autumn floods washed upon the land. European and Euro-American explorers sailed into the Pacific Northwest's inland sea, the Salish Sea, bringing with them not only new ethics, staples, and technologies, but also pathogens that swiftly took to new hosts, the area's indigenous peoples. Lacking immunity to the invasive bacteria and viruses, entire populations of the Coast Salish were decimated. The competing explorers laid claim to the region's vast islands, waters, valleys, and mountains, jostling for possession.

The Spanish were the first to relinquish, but not without leaving testaments of their passage in the form of place names: Guemes, Fidalgo, Rosario, and Padilla, along and within the coastal waters of what is now Skagit County.

The British were next to cede claim to the Skagit and its environs. Through negotiations and finally under threat of war by a fledgling United States, they bowed to the fervor of the rapidly expanding new nation. With the promise of land and opportunity, the belief that Providence was on their side and that it was their manifest destiny to rule from sea to sea, a procession of restless Americans set out to settle this corner of North America called the Oregon Territory.

In 1853, after just seven years under American sovereignty, settlers carved Washington out of this new possession, first as a territory; statehood came in 1889. The year before the new territory was established, "Blanket Bill" Jarman, accompanied by his native Klallam wife, canoed from Port Townsend to Samish Island to become the first permanent non-native resident of what would become Skagit County. The Coast Salish would soon have more new neighbors, for it didn't take

John Scurlock

Samish Island appears to float on the Salish Sea with Lummi Island on the horizon. The Salish Sea refers to the inland waters of the Puget Sound-Georgia Basin ecosystem.

Clear Lake Logging Company train leaves the landing with a load of logs in 1908.

University of Washington Libraries, Special Collections, Darius Kinsey A141.

long for other pioneers to follow. From Canada and California, the Eastern Seaboard, the Southern Appalachians, and the American Heartland, settlers trickled into the fertile flats and timbered islands near the mouth of the Skagit River.

On the wooded headlands and knolls punctuating the area's vast salt marshes, logging camps hastily sprung up. On the prairies of March Point on Fidalgo Island, a new community evolved. But good arable land was limited on the region's rocky and forested bluffs. So, in 1863, pioneers Michael Sullivan and Samuel Calhoun began to dike the surrounding salt marshes to remedy this shortcoming. Though ridiculed by fellow home-steaders, their scheme soon proved successful. Others followed.

Diking continued in earnest for decades afterwards, transforming thousands of acres of marsh and delta into farmland.

New settlements—Skagit City, Edison, La Conner—began to dot the delta of the Skagit. But upriver, commerce was limited. Massive logjams on the river prohibited steamboats from pushing beyond Fir Island downstream of Mount Vernon, and only a muddy military road linked the area with points north and south. By 1879, tenacious workers succeeded in removing the stubborn logjams, giving way for Mount Vernon and points beyond to flourish. And when word spread that a railroad was coming, Anacortes was developed in hope of being the line's economically advantageous terminus. In 1883, with a modest

Northern State Hospital (1909–1976) just east of Sedro-Woolley produced food for patients on its own farm. Dairy barns built in 1921 remain and are now within Northern State Recreation Area, a Skagit County Park.

"Old timers used to say that Sedro-Woolley's economy in the first half of the 20th century sat on a four-legged stool. The first leg was the logging industry, the second was agriculture, the third was Skagit Steel, and the fourth was Northern State Hospital, four miles northeast of town."
—*Skagit River Journal, 2003*

Todd Entrikin

population of just under 3,000, Skagit County was formed. By the 1890s, with the arrival of the railroad and the removal of the logjams, settlement into the region, which had before been but a trickle, transformed into a torrent. Real estate profiteers concocted a land rush on Fidalgo Island.

Upriver, a gold rush was on, leading roads and settlements deeper into the county's eastern fringes. Wilderness valleys that for thousands of years were used primarily by native peoples as trade routes and traversed by just a few intrepid explorers like Alexander Ross were now bustling with fortune seekers.

The growing county and country needed timber and energy. Burlington, Lyman, and Sedro-Woolley burgeoned with

sawmills. Hamilton and Cokedale coughed up coal. Rockport and Marblemount were born to service the growing number of prospectors. And the river itself was soon harnessed for electricity. The first of three dams subduing the mighty waterway was completed in the 1920s.

The nutrient rich soils of the reclaimed salt flats proved ideal for planting peas, oats, beans, spinach, and cabbage. The mild climate and well-irrigated flats were well suited for the growing of seeds. Several decades after A.G. Tillinghast started his seed company on the Padilla Flats in 1885, nearly 95 percent of the country's cabbage seed production came from Skagit County. Nearly a thousand mostly small, family run dairy farms lined the valley during this time as well, making the county a leader in the state in cheese, milk, and butter production.

The Skagit Flats were well suited for growing bulbs, too. In 1906, Mary Brown Stewart imported tulip bulbs from the Netherlands, introducing this showy member of the lily family to Skagit County. While not a food source, the much admired flower provided more than a few families with a viable living and helped establish a sense of local pride and identity through festivals well-heralded throughout the region.

These burgeoning industries needed workers. And from around the country and around the world they came, many bringing their families, deeply altering the ethnic and social fabric of Skagit County. Anacortes attracted fishermen from Croatia and cannery workers from China and the Philippines. Italian laborers were drawn to Concrete's cement factories. The region's woods and sawmills attracted lumbermen from Sweden and Finland, while large numbers of Norwegians,

Lee Mann

Tulips arrived in Skagit Valley near the turn of the 20th century.

Danes, and Japanese took to farming. And when World War II called many of Skagit's sons to the battlefields of Europe and Asia, Mexican Braceros arrived to maintain uninterrupted seed and crop production. Skagit's cultural and ethnic fiber continues to change today as immigrants from North America, Latin America, Eastern Europe, and Asia settle in the valley.

Yet, 100 years after Blanket Bill's arrival, despite thousands of newcomers and the abrupt changes they laid upon the land, the vast majority of Skagit County still remained rural; its coastline largely undeveloped; the upper valley still fairly wild. It helped that a nascent conservation movement at the turn of the 20th century resulted in newly designated national and state forests for over 40 percent of the county's land. State parks were established at Deception Pass and Bay View in the 1920s. Around this time, several municipalities set aside large tracts of land that eventually became community treasures such as the Anacortes Community Forest Lands and Mount Vernon's Little Mountain Park. During the Great Depression, large tracts of private timberland were redrawn for management by the Washington Department of Natural Resources. Hundreds of young men of the Civilian Conservation Corps, FDR's "Tree Army," took up residence in camps outside of Anacortes, Rockport, Lyman, and Marblemount to build trails, campgrounds, and parks and to help restore degraded forests and waterways.

In the 1940s, the Washington Department of Fish and Game began assembling wildlife-rich properties along the Skagit and Samish Rivers for habitat protection. The 1960s and 70s saw a second conservation movement resulting in national park and wilderness protection for some of Skagit County's most spectacular alpine regions, and in a Wild and Scenic River designation for the Skagit River east of Sedro-Woolley. And while March Point, site of the county's first permanent non-native community, now housed a large oil refinery, efforts in the 1950s to transform the expansive eel grass flats and salt marshes to its east into a super industrial center were thwarted. In 1980, over 11,000 acres of previously threatened Padilla Bay were protected within the National Estuarine Research Reserve System.

While various government agencies were responsible for protecting large parcels of Skagit County's lands and waters within the last century, starting in the 1970s a new wave of

Nancy Wagner

Snow Geese take refuge on the Skagit Flats during the winter months.

citizen involvement and community stewardship evolved, greatly enhancing and expanding protected properties. Organizations like The Nature Conservancy, Skagitonians to Preserve Farmland, San Juan Preservation Trust, and Skagit Land Trust, as well as public utilities like Seattle City Light, became pivotal players in helping to protect the region's natural and cultural heritage.

From 1910 until 1970, the county's population modestly grew from 29,000 to 52,000. It seemed as if a balance of sorts had been reached between the area's rural communities and its remaining wild lands. But bigger changes were yet to come to the region and at a much more accelerated rate. Like the rain gradient that spreads across the county from west to east, beginning as light

While snowfall is common during the winter months in Skagit's mountains, the valley usually receives copious amounts of rainfall. However, the occasional snow storm blanketing the low country is not an entirely rare event.

precipitation on the islands within the Olympic Mountain rain shadow and becoming the total inundation of the western slopes of the Cascade Crest, Skagit's population growth saw a progression toward deluge.

From a moderate migration of 300 to 400 people a year in the county's earlier days, newcomers reached an accelerated annual frenzy now 10 times greater. From 1990 to 2000, Skagit County grew by the same number of people, 23,000, as it did from 1910 to 1970. Just as the floodwaters of the mighty Skagit disrupt the land, they also bring nourishment and life to the valley. Skagit County's flood of new residents brings changes too, though not all changes need run counter to the rich landscape that first lured settlers to the area.

While the county has grown rapidly in the past few decades, it still ranks among the most rural and least populated in Washington along the I-5 corridor. Much of its shorelines remain undeveloped. Its fertile valley is still agriculturally viable. Its communities thrive without overflowing into each other. Because so much of the county remains rural, with rehabilitation and sound land practices, its mountains, rivers, and islands may continue to support healthy ecosystems. Skagit County, because of its rural economy and remaining open spaces, offers one of the best

Farmland is central to the valley's character and economy. Citizens supported the use of tax dollars to fund Skagit County's Farmland Legacy Program that buys conservation easements on active farms.

Christine Kitch

chances for conservation of critical wildlife habitat and viable farmland in Western Washington.

Just as resourceful pioneers and first peoples found ways to sustain themselves within the Skagit wilderness, we must find ways to sustain our special quality of life in this region. We must sustain the land that sustains us. Without Skagit's boundless forests, clean waters, flourishing farmlands, and wild coastlines, we lose more than just special aspects of our home, we lose an essential part of ourselves. Consider this: the Skagit River comprises the third largest watershed on the west coast of the continental United States. Yet miraculously, not one major metro-politan area mars its banks. Its headwaters remain untrammeled and wild, protected within national and provincial wilderness parks. Its delta is graced by working farms and wildlife refuges teeming with birds. All five species of Pacific Coast salmon still ply its waters. One of the largest concentrations of Bald Eagles in the Lower 48 can be found along its banks during the winter months, while thousands of Snow Geese and Trumpeter and Tundra Swans take refuge on the river's flats. In the middle of all of this lie Skagit's people. And just like the mighty river, we too are constantly changing, always in flux.

Christine Kitch

Cascades to Chuckanut

Skagit's Forested Shoulders

Molly Doran

Christine Kitch

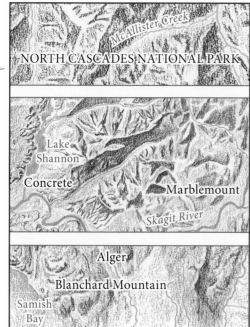

Full-size map on inside cover & page 1

Through millennia, storms from the Pacific Ocean have slammed into the mountains that line the northwest coast of North America, bringing drenching rains and leaving behind valleys of mist. It is a weather cycle that continues to impact a thin band of land between the ocean and mountain crests—the coastal temperate rain forest. Extending from Northern California to Alaska in North America, temperate rain forests are rare on Earth and getting rarer each day. Less than one-fifth of one percent of the world's land can lay claim to its unique, biologically rich features. The only other places with sizeable temperate rain forests are Patagonia in southern Chile and New Zealand.

In turn, this wet, life-nurturing weather has greatly impacted the region's human inhabitants. The Coast Salish tribes and their ancestors lived or hunted in the Skagit forests making use of the forest's great natural wealth. Salmon, cedar, and other staples of the rain forest helped to create a self-sustaining living situation for these first peoples inhabiting the Skagit's rich environment.

However, for the first Euro-American miners and loggers who had a need to both get their equipment into the forests and take their commerce out, the mountainous rain forest was often a barrier to travel. On their heels came new settlements where agriculture

17

Craggy peaks and over 700 glaciers combine to make the North Cascades a world-class mountaineering destination. More than half the glaciers in the 48 states are concentrated in this mountainous wilderness. Its beauty and solitude draw visitors to return time and time again.

Rainfall increases with proximity to the North Cascades. Moist Pacific air meeting the mountains drops more than 100 inches of rain annually in places.

Trillium
Libby Mills

Steve Satushek

was central, yet the farms had to be carved out from the dense lowland forests. The consequences of manipulating elements of nature such as the steady clearing of ancient forest could not be completely known in advance. It is unlikely that these pioneer societies envisioned a time when the forests themselves could be endangered.

Just a little over 100 years later, remnants of old-growth forest are now found mostly in parks and preserves and make up a small fraction of our forest landscape. Yet the magic of coastal temperate rain forests is their regenerating power. Although tropical rain forests hold more biodiversity, our temperate rain forests are able to grow and support the largest concentration of biomass on Earth. Which means, given the right situation, our forests can and do grow back.

Forest to Ocean

Many species depend on the intricate intertwining of forest and ocean. The seven anadromous species of Pacific salmon and trout, which range widely in the North Pacific before returning to their natal coastal rain forest streams to spawn, dramatically

ABOVE LEFT: Wild carrot, or Queen Anne's Lace's name, is derived from Queen Anne of England. The legend goes that she pricked her finger and a drop of blood is responsible for the distinctive tiny purple center of a Queen Anne's Lace flower. ABOVE RIGHT: North America's largest owl, the Great Gray, visits some years from the Cascades to the western lowlands.

demonstrate the reciprocity of forest and sea. As humans, for thousands of years our travels too have followed paths from the forested Cascade Mountain passes to the sea.

The Cascade Mountains, National Park & Forests

The Cascade Range runs 1,000 miles from Northern California to British Columbia. The Skagit River begins in British Columbia's Manning Provincial Park in the northern part of the range. It is a dramatic, rugged landscape of jagged peaks, cascading waterfalls, and steep-forested valleys, many sculpted by glaciers. While the mountains are breathtakingly beautiful, hikers making their way through this precipitous terrain also remark that it is a place for young knees.

It took many years of an ardent, political, and passionate struggle to protect portions of this region as the North Cascades National Park and Ross Lake National Recreational Area. The National Park came into being in 1968. Neighboring the National Park in the Skagit is the immense Mount Baker-Snoqualmie National Forest, one of the most visited national forests in the United States. The U.S. Forest Service is also responsible for the Skagit Wild and Scenic River. Portions of the river east of Sedro-Woolley are managed to protect and enhance its free-flowing condition, water quality, and outstanding natural qualities so that future generations will inherit much of this river in its natural state.

Photo Facing Page, Kevin Thurner »

The North Cascades form the largest and most rugged alpine mountain range in the contiguous United States. Mt. Torment, Mt. Formidable, and Hurricane Peak are some of the place names that help tell this story. Composed of everything from volcanic island arcs and deep ocean sediments, to parts of old continents and even pieces of the deep sub-crustal mantle of the earth, scientists agree that their formation comprises some of the most complex and least understood geology in North America.

Coastal temperate rain forests are distinguished by complex interactions among terrestrial, freshwater, estuarine, and marine systems. Fog aids in providing needed moisture.

Working Forest Lands

Traveling down Skagit's forested shoulders towards the sea, one reaches the working forest lands where there is an active logging industry. The enormous cedars, spruce, firs, and hemlocks of old, clothed in dripping moss, have been harvested and now second- or third-growth forests have taken their place. The single greatest threat to these forests used to be our insatiable appetite for wood; now sprawl and meeting the desires of a fast-expanding population are also taking their toll. Curiously enough, environmentalists and loggers often find themselves fighting for the same long-term goal these days—the need to preserve our forests amidst the mounting threat of development.

Blanchard Mountain

On the seaward edge of the chain of foothills lies one of Skagit's gems—Blanchard Mountain. This forested mountain is largely owned by Washington Department of Natural Resources. It represents a microcosm of the magic, the land-use complexity and the threats to Skagit forests. It is the only place left in Puget Sound where the coastal rain forest wedged against the Cascade Mountains connects to the sea. It is a beloved recreational area in the midst of growing population centers. Yet its designation as an industrial forest has also helped to maintain a working forest base, instead of subdivisions, in the chain of forested foothills running up the valley. A complex, passionate debate about logging or not logging on Blanchard has been on-going. This debate will be repeated up and down the valley as our community comes to grips with choices we must make as new threats to forests and biodiversity march closer. Forests—even coastal temperate rain forests with the most prodigious growth on earth—are not forever if we pave them over.

Seventy-two people on a cedar stump 60 feet in circumference, Sedro-Woolley, Washington, 1890. Photo: Frank Le Roche.

Early settlers encountered immense trees in the Skagit. Today, it is hard to imagine that only a little over 100 years ago, the routes that mark many of our daily commutes were once situated amidst stands of seemingly endless forest.

Tony Jewell

BOTTOM RIGHT: The Hegg-Benson Trail on Skagit Land Trust's Barr Creek Conservation Area located at the base of Sauk Mountain.

LEFT: Students on a month-long expedition with the National Outdoor Leadership School (NOLS) traverse a meadow in the Glacier Peak Wilderness Area.

BOTTOM LEFT: Sauk Mountain with an elevation of 5,537 feet is one of the most beloved land marks in the Skagit Valley. The zigzagging climb to take in the 360-degree views from the summit is a Skagit rite of passage for local hikers.

White Pine Cone
Brenda Cunningham

Steve Philbrick

Rosemary Seifreid

After devastating fires in the Midwest, in 1891, Congress established forest reserves including huge parcels in Washington State. Fire watchers and their lookouts soon followed. This site on Lookout Mountain is intact and usable for those who make the lofty 4,500 climb from the Cascade River.

Photo Next Page: Pat Buller »

Mountains in Fog. "What goes up must come down." But how? The pilot tried six airports before finally corkscrewing down through a hole in the clouds over Shaw Island, in neighboring San Juan County, to land a very relieved photographer. —Lee Mann

LEE MANN, *Nature Photographer*

"I love the Skagit; it's incredible," says Lee Mann. "You've got mountains on one side and ocean on the other." Having lived in Skagit since 1965, Lee considers himself lucky to be able to share this beauty with the greater world while doing what he loves most, photographing nature.

For over 35 years, camera bags in tow, Lee has trekked to the top of mountains, rambled through remote desert canyons, and walked across vast sub-Arctic prairies in search of beauty and light. It's a passion, he admits, that requires a certain way of looking at things. "It isn't enough for me to see a thing in its form, but to also see it in its light." Indeed, Lee returns many times to capture a passing moment. It's an outlook he attributes, in part, to his boyhood in the Sultan Basin in Skykomish. "We were out in the boonies. I spent a lot of time alone as a kid playing in the woods."

After graduating high school in Sultan and serving in the Navy, Lee attended Western Washington University where he became an avid mountaineer and discovered photography. He was one of the first members of the North Cascades Conservation Council and took up the call, with a handful of others, to establish the North Cascades National Park. Lee remembers the warnings of his father and grandfather, both loggers. "They saw that timber was coming to an end, that we would need some other economic base for this community." For Lee, the formation of the National Park was not only about preserving natural spaces but was also a much needed shift in thinking about our collective future.

Lee went on to become a popular eighth-grade language arts and social studies teacher for over a decade before eventually turning to photography full time. Connecting the two lives, he explains, "When you're teaching you can change a few people a whole lot; when you publish a photograph you can change a whole lot of people just a little bit. It's part of communicating an appreciation of the beauty around us and having an impact on thinking."

—*Patricia Chambers*

Suzanne Fogarty

Lee Mann in his photography studio in Sedro-Woolley, Washington.

Lee Mann

Mountain Wildflowers. Looking at the Sisters Range from a very fragile, very isolated, very secret ridge. Sorry, you will have to sign an oath in blood to get the directions from me! —Lee Mann

29

Rosemary Seifreid

Lee Mann

Erin McKay

Michael Kirshenbaum

The Cascade Range supports over 300 species of wildlife. Deer, black bear, and mountain goats are common. Mountain lions, bobcats, grizzly bear and wolves are present but rarely seen. TOP RIGHT: Place names help tell the story of the North Cascades' ruggedness and beauty: hikers summit Magic Mountain and look at Forbidden Peak in the distance.

Barr Creek
Connecting Wildlife Habitat

Christine Kitch

Skagit Land Trust's Barr Creek Conservation Area at the base of Sauk Mountain connects critical low elevation wildlife habitat on Sauk Mountain to higher elevation public lands and forests. The network of protected lands in this area is considered large enough to recover populations of 22 animal species considered Species of Special Concern in Washington State. The Trust's purchase of this property took three years to complete and was assisted by the Washington Department of Natural Resources, the U.S. Fish and Wildlife Service, the Washington Department of Fish and Wildlife, and almost 200 individual donors.

The property, also called "Kermit's Woods," hosts a multitude of benefits. It is an older forest of fir and cedar with an unusual amount of high quality wildlife habitat including a pristine creek and eagle night roost. The forest will soon reach a condition suitable for Marbled Murrelet habitat. It lies within the Skagit River Bald Eagle Natural Area, designated as such by The Nature Conservancy due to the hundreds of Bald Eagles who gather each winter to feed on returning salmon. The Hegg-Benson Trail traversing the property is the beginning of the old east-flank Sauk Mountain trail. This trail was constructed to reach the now defunct fire lookout built in 1928. The lookout was notoriously hard to reach because of the steep trail that rose over 5,000 feet up Sauk Mountain's rocky ridges. In the 1950s logging roads enabled easier access on the west side of Sauk Mountain where today's popular hike up Sauk Mountain begins.

—*Molly Doran*

Brenda Cunningham

The mysterious Marbled Murrelet nests in old-growth trees up to 50 miles inland at night, yet feeds in the ocean during the day.

Bobcat

Steve Philbrick

Trillium and Bunchberry

Pat Buller

Violet Cortinarius

Phil Green

MIKE JANICKI, *Logger*

In Mike Janicki's perfect world, the rule would be: "Nobody gets to waste wood." This may seem an unusual statement from the president of a logging company whose market is wood users, but Janicki is adamant. "We need to worry about what energy we are taking away from our grandchildren."

Janicki has another reason for pushing society to build an atmosphere of conservation: he loves forests. He does not want to see forests turned into housing developments. Janicki says, "My family has been here 100 years. Over that time you see trends, and the biggest trend is that the trees grow back unless there's a house there."

In the 1940s, Mike Janicki's grandfather started a shake mill in Sedro–Woolley. The innovative, industrious family spirit that founded this first Janicki-owned business has since spawned companies such as Janicki Logging and Construction and Janicki Industries, an aerospace, marine, and transportation-related manufacturing business. Today, most third-generation Janickis and their spouses are officers and directors in the family's enterprises. Janicki Logging is run by Mike and his brother Rob. One of the elixirs of the Janickis' success has been the attitude of cooperation instilled in them by their mother Annie. "The rule is that all are treated equally," says Mike. "If you're making decisions about what's best for the family, you consider everybody's needs."

Perhaps not coincidentally, Mike's views on forest management also consider more than just the well-being of a single tree. "A forest stand has to have diversity, and not just of tree species. For example, it has to have the right bugs and healthy soil. When we have an invasive disease we have to fight it as if it were a forest fire. Yet, if the ecosystem is healthy, it can take care of its stressors. When you pay attention to this you get better trees. Besides," he adds, "what's best for the tree is usually what's best economically."

—*Molly Doran*

Suzanne Fogarty

Steve Satushek

Western slope forests produce an astonishing quantity of plant mass and are unbeatable in the world for growing trees.

Wade Clark Jr.

Sword Fern

Nathan Cranston

Shooting Star

Pat Buller

Western Toad

Steve Satushek

White-tailed Ptarmigan

Todd Entrikin

Turkeytail Fungus

Diane Bednarz

Steve Satushek

"A RIVER RUNS DEEP IN MY MEMORY, AS IT ONCE RAN DEEP IN MY LIFE—THE SKAGIT RIVER, in northern Washington. As a boy I lived in a small village right on the Skagit. My bedroom faced the river, maybe 100 yards away and for many years I fell asleep to the deep, steady sigh of its flowing, as much a physical sensation as a sound.

In the light of day, the river took on a dark emerald tint borrowed from the spruces, pines, and firs that bristled down the slopes of the Cascades to its very banks. Though not much given to aesthetic reflection, I thought even then that it was beautiful. My friends and I fished it for steelhead and trout, but left the salmon alone as they fought their way upstream to spawn. The Bald Eagles were less compassionate. They congregated just upstream from Marblemount, where we changed buses on our long drive to school, and we sometimes played truant for a day to watch them hunt—skimming just inches above the water, then lifting their thrashing prey to the topmost branches of a tree.

It was beautiful, the river, but no ornament. We were constantly warned of its dangers, and inevitably a boy from our village drowned. This added a deeper shade to its color, a darker timbre to its voice, but I loved it no less. When I finally left, I had trouble sleeping. Nights without that breathing presence seemed so hollow, airless. I still miss it."

—*Tobias Wolff*

Tobias Wolff is the author of eight books and the editor of The Vintage Book of American Short Stories. Among his honors are the PEN/Malamud Award and the Rea Award, both for excellence in the short story, the Los Angeles Times Book Prize, and the PEN/Faulkner Award. Among his works is This Boy's Life, a memoir of his growing up in Skagit County, Washington. He lives in Northern California and teaches at Stanford University.

The River

Our Home, Our Highway, Our Pantry

Libby Mills

Steve Satushek

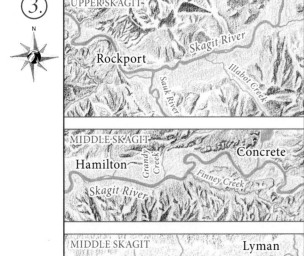

Full-size map on inside cover & page 1

The river moves; its waters swirl, swell, and sing. Turquoise blue, it refracts light into colors the winter sky rarely sees. Glacial ice in the North Cascades grinds the mountains to "glacial flour," depositing particles into the river's headwaters and producing its hue. From the southwest, a winter storm roars in, dumping a deluge onto last week's snow pack. On the Sauk River, a major tributary to the Skagit, the water grows brown, growling as it tears at the banks, breaking them down, feeding on timber and woody debris. In a cataclysmic event, the river's path crosses the valley, creating vital habitat for salmon. The river's flooding erodes and carries away large trees to scour pools that tiny salmon fry use for refuge in high water. Heavy current pulls fresh gravel and cobbles out of the riverbanks and lays them in the riverbed for spawning fish to use. Large woody-debris jams lead to new islands, and, with time, new forests emerge in the floodplain.

So the forests and their demise in the flooding Skagit River lead to renewed salmon habitat. In turn, marine-derived nitrogen moving upstream in the form of adult home-ward-migrating salmon feeds the region's forests as salmon carcasses decompose on the banks and tree roots take up their nutrients.

Lee Mann

John Scurlock

Christine Kitch

The Skagit River is more than 160 miles long and the third largest river on the West Coast of the contiguous United States. It provides about 20 percent of the fresh water flowing into Puget Sound, nearly 10 billion gallons a day. The Skagit supports one of the Lower 48's last strongholds of salmon as well as rich farmland and habitat for many species of wildlife and birds. Portions of it were designated a Wild and Scenic River in 1978.

The Skagit sits sandwiched between the Pacific Northwest's largest metropolitan areas, Seattle and Vancouver, B.C. Yet despite the pressure from development, Skagit County remains the most sparsely populated county in Puget Sound. Several dozen private non-profits and government agencies are helping to conserve the natural systems and resource lands of this important watershed. TOP RIGHT: The Sauk River, home to the Sauk-Suiattle Tribe.

ABOVE: Humpback (pink) salmon return to the Skagit in odd-numbered years and vie for habitat and females over the cobbled riverbed. The arching hump of the males' backs marks the end of their two-year life cycle and develops as they prepare to spawn. RIGHT: A chum salmon on its spawning grounds will soon die and become part of the ecosystem's food chain.

Salmon are a keystone species on which many other species at least partially depend for survival. All stages of salmon, from eggs and fry to adult fish living and dead, provide food to over 137 species of wildlife. These range from the salmon's own newly hatched offspring (baby salmon must have dead adult salmon to eat!) to Bald Eagles, Harlequin Ducks, and 58 other bird species, and from killer whales and black bears to river otters and 22 other mammal species. Huge reductions in historical wild salmon runs have left our river ecosystems starving for the nutrients once arriving on abundant wild salmon runs. We need salmon as the engine to a rich ecosystem of many habitats, both terrestrial and aquatic.

Still, the Skagit River boasts a great diversity of plants and wildlife. Beaver, muskrat, deer, elk, and coyote all find a home on the river's edge. So do a mosaic of young and old trees and shrubs—exactly the world a migratory songbird seeks. Surviving the perils of flight from Central America and Mexico, Warbling Vireo, Yellow Warbler, Swainson's Thrush, and Black-headed

A place of constant change, the river rolling back and forth in its bed across the valley creates a natural environment for salmon to reproduce. Each of the Skagit's five species of salmon uses a different size gravel or small cobble for spawning. They divide up the river's waters for places to spawn, both in space and in time. Chinook salmon, the largest, use the heaviest current in the main stem and largest tributaries of the river. Coho salmon and steelhead swim far up the Skagit, Sauk, and Cascade Rivers to spawn in the uppermost tributaries, while smaller sockeye salmon swim to their ancestral waters of Baker Lake to spawn along lake shores and lake tributaries. Every season, historically, would host another migration of adult salmon into the Skagit, feeding the ecosystem, including the first peoples.

LEFT: A Red-breasted Sapsucker pecks feeding wells in the sap-layer of trees. These birds regularly lap up sap of red alders, willows, and conifers with their stiffly-fringed tongue. *Libby Mills*

RIGHT: a juvenile Glaucous-winged Gull, Great Blue Heron, and immature Bald Eagles crowd around salmon carcasses on the upper Skagit River. Eagles eat half a pound to a pound of salmon daily to meet their energy requirements. *Bryce Mann*

Grosbeak fill the May air with their flutey and whistled songs. In late December, hundreds of Bald Eagles crowd the banks of the middle and upper river watershed, feasting on chum salmon carcasses. American Dippers and Belted Kingfishers, Harlequin Ducks, and Common Mergansers, Spotted Sandpipers, and Osprey make a vital part of their salmon-dependent living along the river. Little-understood Black Swifts arrive from South America to nest behind waterfalls in the river's steep mountain headwaters. Their cousins the Vaux's Swifts seek old hollow tree snags to raise their young through the long insect-rich summer evenings.

oceanspray, Libby Mills

The river also moves people. The human story to survive, flourish, and grow is a familiar one in the West. First peoples were hunters and fishermen, shellfish gatherers, and forest foragers, afoot and afloat. Community tradition and experimentation taught them the strength of the Pacific yew and oceanspray's wood, the nutritional value in young salmonberry leaves and nettles, the durability of the salal berry that could be dried for winter use. Devil's club provided much in the pharmacy. Western red cedar, which grew best in the wet soils, provided bark fiber for clothing, mat weaving, and baskets, while its even-grained wood could be worked into longhouses, storage boxes, and canoes.

The next waves of humanity were trappers and miners. Then came loggers, settlers, farmers, and commercial fishermen. It was the century of extraction and settlement. They came to make a life or find fortune. They founded the towns and resource economies

Wade Clark Jr.

Steve Philbrick

Libby Mills

LEFT: Clear snowmelt cascades through steep mountains to form the headwaters of the vast Skagit watershed. Nine months of abundant rainfall supports rich moss growth. CENTER: The American Dipper uses moss to insulate its nest. The Dipper dives under water to eat insect larvae, salmon eggs, and tiny fish. RIGHT: A male Warbling Vireo sings from its nest. Migratory songbirds feeding their hungry nestlings are a major force of natural insect pest control. By mid-August, the vireos begin their migration to a small range in Mexico and Central America wintering in woodlands and shade coffee plantations.

of today. They exported minerals, logged the huge trees, fished hard on the salmon runs, diked the river, seeded the captured delta farmlands and sheparded in the resource economy of today's Skagit. Today's wave of humanity often comes to the Skagit River drawn by her resources and beauty. The new settler is often seeking an edge between the wilderness and civilization. Today's logger harvests second- or third-growth stands and considers the effects on various aspects of the forest ecosystem, including biological diversity, nutrient cycling, and forest health. New forest-related livelihoods include everything from furniture maker and chainsaw sculptor to stream restoration specialist. Traditional farmers, too, are considering new paths. As global environmental pressures on traditional farming

Douglas-fir,
Libby Mills

practices increase, many are seeking local markets, including local restaurants and schools, growing organic vegetables and berries for the nation, considering conservation easements to protect the family farm, and incorporating value-added aspects to diversify their businesses.

Many travelers come here to recreate. The river's visitors are riding the rapids in dory, raft, or kayak, birding the forests along the river's edge for tropical visitors and resident songsters. They are biking the old rail lines turned to trails, hiking the trails that climb into the peaks and snow.

With portions of the river designated a National Wild and Scenic River in 1978, the Skagit's fisheries, wildlife, beauty, and recreation potential have captured a lot of attention. A map of land ownership along the middle and upper Skagit River from

Volunteers for groups such as the Skagit Fisheries Enhancement Group, The Skagit Conservation District, Skagit Land Trust, and The Nature Conservancy help with stream monitoring, noxious weed removal, and replanting native trees and shrubs along river shorelines.

Sedro-Woolley to Marblemount shows the ongoing work to reassemble an open floodplain of properties where the river is able to run free. Thanks to active conservation work, dozens of miles of riverbank now allow the river to do its essential work naturally—with salmon and wildlife habitat helped along by replanting of native vegetation.

A Saturday and a shovel are part of the solution to moving the Skagit River forward to reach its potential again. There are many conservation and stewardship projects to join, led by legions of volunteers who want to reshape a more natural Skagit for generations to come. Partnerships provide a common forum for protecting salmon habitat and restoring the natural health of this mighty river system. A healthy fishery is the indicator of a healthy watershed. Working to get one, you get the other.

Steve Philbric

ABOVE: A refreshing summer rain falls on cattle grazing near the St. Martin and St. Francis Episcopal Church in Rockport on the upper Skagit River near Sauk Mountain. FACING PAGE: Top Left, A chain saw carver puts the final touches on an animated bear sculpture in a 4th of July contest in Sedro-Woolley. BOTTOM LEFT: The Government Bridge crosses the free-flowing Sauk River. UPPER RIGHT: The forested slope behind popular Cascadian Farm is permanently protected with a conservation easement donated to Skagit Land Trust. LOWER RIGHT: Farming in the up river area is assisted by hot summers and upwards of 85

Steve Philbrick

© Natalie Fobes, www.fobesphoto.com

Lee Mann

Benj Drummond

ABOVE LEFT: An adult Bald Eagle calls from a low alder branch by the river. The annual Bald Eagle Festival centered in Concrete celebrates wintering eagles. In 1976, The Nature Conservancy and the Washington Department of Fish and Wildlife created the Skagit River Bald Eagle Natural Area and have since brought in dozens of partners to help protect eagle habitat in the upper Skagit.

BOTTOM RIGHT: North Cascades Institute and the U.S. Forest Service train volunteers to point out eagles to winter visitors and work to educate the public on how to enjoy eagles without driving them off the river.

LEFT: Eagles compete for food through the shortest days of winter, then return to Alaska and Canada in spring, showing pair bonding behavior before returning north to nest in February.

TOP RIGHT: Summer on the river brings visitors out to enjoy a raft ride.

Salmonberry, Libby Mills

Phil Green

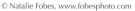

ABOVE CENTER: Salmon fry hide from predators and find food in the pools and submerged roots of large woody debris. **ABOVE RIGHT:** Chum salmon will be utilized right down to tooth and bone by mammals, birds, fish, and invertebrates recycling their marine-derived nutrients through the ecosystem.

SHIRLEY SOLOMON, *Salmon Warrior*

In the fight to save the Skagit River salmon, there are many homegrown warriors, but very few who hail from South Africa. In the 1960s, Shirley left South Africa and immigrated to the United States, where she earned a graduate degree in environmental planning from Arizona State University. She has served as a consultant to tribes, government, and private land owners throughout the west. Shirley was a project director for Northwest Renewable Resources Center and Long Live the Kings (a non-profit dedicated to salmon recovery). It was in that capacity that Solomon fell in love with the "Magic Skagit," and realized her life's true calling: to facilitate a collaborative effort for the recovery of the Skagit salmon runs.

In 1997, she cofounded Skagit Watershed Council, a community partnership focused on the voluntary restoration and preservation of salmon habitat. Today, she still serves as the Council's president and represents the Skagit Watershed Council as a policy-setter for salmon recovery across Puget Sound. Talk to Shirley Solomon about Skagit salmon and you will hear optimism—notable for a woman with an admittedly upstream battle. But Shirley is also pragmatic, and acknowledges the often-challenging job of bringing together stakeholders with very different viewpoints to accomplish a common goal. With her understanding smile, she remarks that it's sometimes hard to get one family to agree on dinner; so, she says, imagine building consensus with farmers, fisherman, tribes, and various government agencies at the table.

Working passionately at the state, regional, and local levels to help salmon recovery, Shirley says that all of us need to remember that the fate of these magnificent creatures rests with each and every one of us. —*Megan Scott O'Bryan*

Kirsten Morse

Michelle Blaine

"Thanks to Tony Morefield"

What do you learn
on the river?
Free boots
always leak.
—Robert Sund

Diane Bednarz

Christine Kitch

Many come to the Skagit River for her solace and beauty—to recreate, fish for food, or to find peace in a quiet day. LEFT: Abundant tart berries of Oregon grape feed birds and mammals at the base of a red cedar.

"Thanks to Tony Morefield" and "Herons and Swallows" (pg. 50) by Robert Sund are from Poems from Ish River Country: Collected Poems and Translations by Robert Sund, Shoemaker & Hoard, Publishers, Washington D.C., 2004, and used with gratitude and permission of the Robert Sund Poet's House *robertsundpoetshouse.org*.

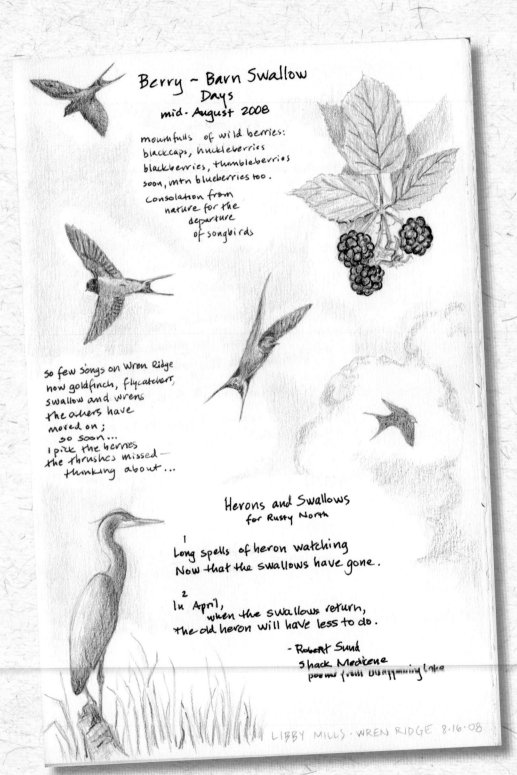

Berry ~ Barn Swallow Days
mid. August 2008

mouthfulls of wild berries:
blackcaps, huckleberries
blackberries, thimbleberries
soon, mtn blueberries too.
Consolation from
nature for the
departure
of songbirds

So few songs on Wren Ridge
now goldfinch, flycatchers,
swallow and wrens
the others have
moved on;
   so soon...
I pick the berries
the thrushes missed —
   thinking about...

Herons and Swallows
for Rusty North

1
Long spells of heron watching
Now that the swallows have gone.

2
In April,
   when the swallows return,
the old heron will have less to do.

   – Robert Sund
   Shack Medicine
   poems from Disappearing Lake

LIBBY MILLS · WREN RIDGE 8·16·08

Barn Swallows migrate to Skagit Valley from as far away as Argentina and Chile. In mid-July the parents tirelessly feed their insect-hungry broods to prepare for the journey south.

Libby Mills

Wild Blackberry, a native prickly vine, is closely watched in fruiting season by berry-gatherers for a sweet tasty reward. Only the female flowers produce the fruit. You'll be disappointed finding only the male-flowered shrubs!

Libby Mills

Great Blue Herons are abundant on Padilla Bay. Skagit Land Trust protects the land and a heronry that produces hundreds of the tall birds annually.

Thomas Plank

A naturalist's illustrated field journal is both a tool for recording important observations in the natural world and a refuge for a naturalist to slow down, look, listen, write, draw, and open the senses to become a better observer.

Steve Philbrick

Beaver activity on the river and its tributaries has many positive effects. By cutting willow and cottonwood, beavers stimulate dense sprouting and help stabilize the shoreline. Their dams produce a diversity of habitats for amphibians, birds, and other animals. By slowing and trapping the runoff of water and silt they benefit salmon.

One of the last big farms in the Skagit upriver community was protected from subdivision through a unique partnership initiated by land owners Barb Trask and Ger van den Engh, shown right taking a walk on their farm Elysium.

Suzanne Fogarty

John Scurlock

BARBARA TRASK AND GER VAN DEN ENGH, *Landowners*

In 2007, one of the last big farms in the Skagit upriver community was protected from subdivision in a partnership among the landowners, Barbara Trask and Ger van den Engh; Skagit Land Trust; and the Washington State Salmon Recovery Funding Board (SRFB). The 127-acre property was originally a dairy farm that was bought by a developer who had subdivided the land for residences. A paved street was put in and lots were put up for sale.

Barb and Ger discovered the property when looking for a small farm to purchase. "The idea of rescuing the property from development had enormous appeal to us," says Barb. Located on a bend in the Skagit River near Birdsview, the property is about half open farmland and half woodland. It includes a mile of forested river shoreline with extensive gravel bars: high quality habitat for chinook salmon, a federally-listed Endangered Species. Beyond the shoreline lies excellent grazing land for livestock, who often share the area with elk.

Suzanne Fogarty

Barb and Ger ultimately purchased nine lots, reactivated the farm, and took out the paved road. With the assistance of Skagit Land Trust, they placed a conservation easement on 112 acres to conserve the wildlife habitat. They donated over half the value of this easement, and SRFB chipped in for the rest. This permanent preservation agreement allows residential use of the existing farmhouse and ongoing agriculture on the farmland but extinguishes all other residential development rights within the 112-acre conservation easement. A fourth partner, Skagit Fisheries Enhancement Group, is now working with Barb and Ger to plant native trees that restore more of this floodplain habitat to its natural state.

When they are not busy with their farm in the Skagit, Barb and Ger are active research scientists in Seattle. Skagit Land Trust's conservation director Martha Bray says, "Barb and Ger are inspiring. They are choosing to make a difference in the world. We are so grateful for the vision they have."

—*Molly Doran*

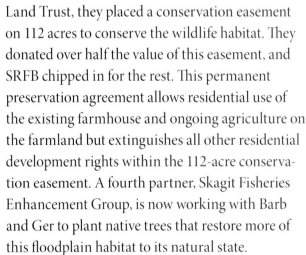

Skagit Land Trust

Skagit Land Trust charter
member Jerry Haegele places
a sign at the Trust's Hurn
Field property near Concrete.
LEFT: Rocky Mountain Elk
are commonly viewed from
a pullout at Hurn Field on
Highway 20.

Lee Mann

Steve Satushek

RIGHT: Pacific Northwest old growth forests support greater biomass (living
matter) per acre than any other place on earth. ABOVE: Douglas-fir and
western hemlock overshadow a forest floor of maidenhair fern, twisted stalk,
tiger lily, and spring beauty.

Kevin Thurner

Bryce Mann

The Skagit River is our home. Our highway, and our pantry.

The river has a language that is understood by all of us and if you listen closely
you can understand too, the music that it's singing to us
and the language that it is speaking to us.

—Vi "taqʷšəblu" *Hilbert*
Huchoosedah: Traditions of the Heart, 1995

VI HILBERT
Upper Skagit Elder

Upper Skagit archives

Mary Randlett

At the time Vi was born in 1918, the Baker River flowed directly into the Skagit, unimpeded by the two dams that stand today, the first being built in 1925. LEFT: Upper Skagit Tribal men in Canoe on Baker River, c. early 1900s. RIGHT: Vi Hilbert in 2000.

Vi "taqʷšəblu" Hilbert, honored elder of the Upper Skagit Tribe and a woman revered by many, was born July 24, 1918, near the Skagit River at Lyman. As an only child, Hilbert's earliest years were shaped by close contact with the forests and rivers of the upper Skagit watershed.

In 1967, while living in Seattle, Hilbert turned back to her early years on the Skagit as she began her life's work: the preservation of Lushootseed, the language of her childhood and that of Puget Sound's Coast Salish people, because, as she said, *It is work the Creator wrapped around me to do.*

Hilbert's diligence in documenting her people's culture and literature in their native tongue has resulted in over twenty books, countless workshops around the globe, and the respect of many as she has freely shared her knowledge. She is a Living Treasure of Washington (1989), a recipient of both the National Heritage Fellowship (1994) and Humanities Washington Award (2006). As she marks her 90th year, Vi shares the following thoughts on the place of her birth.

I grew up with parents who honored one other. My father was a logger and a fisherman so wherever there was a job, that is where we lived. We didn't have a home, we lived wherever there was a shelter. But my mother knew how to make a home with very few things. We didn't have a car. We had a canoe. So anytime we went someplace, we either had to walk, or we went by canoe. It held everything we needed.

When I was two or three, my dad was hired to get men who were strong on the water. They worked in canoes along the Baker River, pushing cedar bolts free from obstacles and moving them down to the mill in Concrete. My mother cooked for my dad's crew. And I got to go along, just enjoying the world that I got to share. It was hard work with many risks but the men knew how to be on the water.

My most vivid memory is living on the Skagit River between Lyman and Hamilton. That was my friend, that area. I can feel the place. It was a good place. These memories are very precious. A way of life without a grocery store, a good clean life that was shared. All of our people knew how to do this. My people honored what the river provided. The land and the river upriver, and the land and the saltwater downriver.

—Theresa Trebon

Quotations are from two oral histories conducted with Vi Hilbert: February 2007 by Theresa Trebon; August 2008 by Theresa Trebon and Carmen Pastores-Joe.

Christine Kitch

Greater Skagit Flats

Living in the Flood Plain

Howard Armstrong

Dave Smith

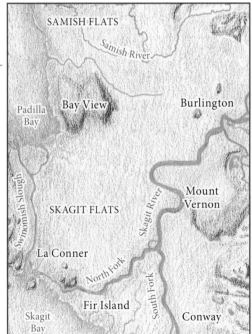

Full-size map on inside cover & page 1

The Samish and Skagit Flats lie in the floodplains of the mighty Skagit River and its much smaller neighbor the Samish. Built of sediments transported by the river over thousands of years, the flats were once covered with primeval forests of cedar, hemlock, and fir. At their edges, vast marshes teemed with shorebirds, waterfowl, and salmon fry. As Euro-American settlers arrived in the area in the 1860s, they brought the desire for commerce with them. First the logging camps came; trees were felled and the stumps removed. The waters of the Puget Sound-Georgia Basin played a key role as timber and lumber were shipped all over the world from its ports. Towns such as La Conner, Burlington, and Mount Vernon grew up on the edges of this delta landscape, positioned to capitalize on the logging camps dotting the waterways. Each town was an autonomous commercial center with post office, school, stores, and both temporary and permanent housing.

These small towns easily nestled on the edge of the river or bay alongside the ebb and flow of the tides and flood-prone river. With the clear-cutting of thousands of acres of timber, much viable land for farming was available by the 1870s. The marshes were diked to make additional rich delta farmland, and the rise of homesteading, subsistence farming, and agriculture grew. However, as the towns grew in population, their "nestling"

57

Martin Burwash

Kelli Christoferson

Kirsten Morse

Corwin Fergus

Agriculture is the number one industry in Skagit County with 93,000 acres of active farmland. ABOVE MIDDLE: Washington State Governor Christine Gregoire encourages sandbaggers on the shoreline of the Skagit River as it reaches flood stage. ABOVE RIGHT: In addition to food products, agriculture provides habitat for thousands of swans, snow geese, and dabbling ducks and expansive open space for the community. BOTTOM RIGHT: The Skagit River created the rich soil of the Skagit Flats, but it can also cause extensive damage to property and structures located in the flood plain.

became more difficult, and today the towns and cities of the flats share a complex relationship with the dynamic Skagit River and its flooding. Every few years the river sends a wet warning against further building in the floodplain—a hard message for human enterprise bursting at the seams and eager to expand, yet a fortuitous message for the valley's agriculture, wildlife, and rural character.

As one would expect with such change, some species gained while others lost. Fish were among those heavily affected by the significant habitat changes wrought by humankind, with salmon and many native fish species struggling to remain viable populations. Work to save these fish populations continues to be a difficult and vital challenge as we struggle to find a landscape balance in the floodplain. Birds, however, fared somewhat bet-

The quintessential "Skagit Flats view" looking east across the Samish Flats to the entrance of the Skagit River Valley. Organizations such as Skagitonians to Preserve Farmland, Skagit County's Farmland Legacy Program, and Skagit Land Trust protect farmland throughout the Skagit.

ter—their relationship with the altered landscape took root over time. Although the cutting of the forests and draining of wetlands displaced many thousands of birds, the pastures and crop fields presented opportunities for large numbers of waterfowl and raptors. Today, despite the pressures of human population growth and development, the fertile valley continues to provide food and a home for both people and birds. It is a relationship that demon-strates a unique aspect that is part of the magic of the Skagit. To illustrate this magic, we will focus on some of the avian wonders that share the valley with us and on our relationship to them.

Snow Geese

In October each year, thousands of Lesser Snow Geese return from a season of breeding on Wrangel Island off the coast of

Christine Kitch

Lesser Snow Geese cover a field on Fir Island. The color on the head is rust stain from the soil as they probe for carrots and other food.

Christine Kitch

Jerry Eisner

ABOVE: The Skagit Flats is one of the most popular areas for birding in the state. Wildlife viewing has a profound impact on Skagit's rural economy. Over $1 billion is spent annually in Washington on wildlife watching activities. Skagit is one of the state's wildlife viewing gems. RIGHT: Male Marsh Wrens build multiple nests in marsh reeds and sing to attract females and establish their territories.

Siberia. The flock has been gone since March. Their return signals a change from autumn to winter. Wave after wave of white and black geese honking fills the Skagit skies. The geese land in the fields to feed on grass, grains, and vegetables left after harvesting. The birds will work hard to gain back the fat they lost during nesting and migration. Seeing these ghostly waves of geese makes it difficult to believe that their population was once down to a few thousand birds. Now more than 100,000 Lesser Snow Geese winter on the deltas of the Skagit and Fraser Rivers. In fact, the population has reached the point where they are out-eating their welcome on some of the farms of nearby Fir Island, a preferred feeding area. To help solve this problem, the Washington Depart-

ment of Fish and Wildlife is leading a task force of area residents, state representatives, farmers, hunters, and conservationists in an attempt to reconcile wildlife and agricultural needs.

Trumpeter Swans

Soon after the arrival of the Snow Geese, a primordial trumpeting announces the arrival of the legendary Trumpeter Swans. Hunted for their meat and feathers, Trumpeters were thought to be extinct by the late 1800s, but have become one of the great success stories for conservation. On most winter weekends, these four-foot tall birds and their slightly smaller cousins, Tundra Swans and Snow Geese, become the focus of birders and photographers

At over 20 pounds, the Trumpeter Swan is North America's largest waterfowl. ABOVE: A small group of the approximately 1,800 Trumpeter Swans that winter in the Skagit Valley fly low over the fields where they feed.

who travel from afar to watch the birds as they graze and eat the remains of unharvested corn, potatoes, carrots, and whatever else is available in their Skagit winter home. When the swans leave in late February or early March to follow ancient migration patterns to the Alaskan tundra, the fields that fed them so well all winter will be tilled and planted with crops to feed their human residents.

Raptors

There are few places in North America better than the Samish and Skagit Flats in winter for enjoying avian predators, known as raptors. Raptors from Canada and Alaska migrate south and join the local birds to eat the abundant supply of voles, other small mammals, and smaller birds in the area. Rough-legged Hawks from the north hover over open fields or join local Red-tailed Hawks to perch on power wires and poles and to scan the grasses below for their small, furry food. Northern Harriers by day and Short-eared Owls by both day and night rock, dip, and float over the vole-rich, grass-covered fields looking for a meal. Peregrine Falcons, back from the brink of extinction, snatch ducks or shorebirds in mid-air dives at speeds approaching 200 miles per hour.

Shorebirds

Just as raptors are respected for their ferocity and power, shorebirds are admired for their speed and agility. These long-winged, fast, graceful birds are mostly very long-range fliers. They streak through the Skagit in April and May on their northward

Barney Lake

John Scurlock

Skagit Land Trust owns 95 acres in the Barney Lake area near Mount Vernon. Barney Lake is well known for its wintering waterfowl habitat, including Trumpeter Swans, and provides important flood water storage for the community.

A rare category of wetland, the story of Barney Lake's protection demonstrates how a community comes together to protect beloved land. The first acquisition was a gift from Don Parry and Vicki Soderberg Parry in 1995, followed by gifting of adjacent land by Ken Willis and Linda Speck in 1997. The Trust then purchased more wetlands and forest with a grant from the U.S. Fish and Wildlife Service matched by community donations.

migration, only stopping long enough to refuel as their instincts drive them to hurry on to their breeding grounds on the tundra of northern Canada and Alaska. They return on their more leisurely southward migration in August through October. For some farmers in the area, these shorebird populations—such as plovers and sandpipers including Dunlin, Dowichers, and Yellowlegs—could mean new economic opportunities. As part of a three-year pilot program called Farming for Wildlife, three La Conner-area farmers are currently partnering with The Nature Conservancy to convert parts of their fields into habitat for shorebirds. If the program proves successful it may expand to other farms, creating new wetlands for the declining shorebird populations (See page 67).

Home for People and Birds

For generations, birds and people have shared the area. This ability to share and be shaped by nature is nothing new to Skagit communities. Even as these communities grapple with complex issues such as salmon recovery, flood control, and loss of wetlands and farmland to pavement, nature remains the silent but most powerful voice in the discussion. It continues to remind us that living in the floodplain means living with nature. Alongside the many stories of species decline and habitat loss, the story of birds on the flats of Skagit County is a reminder that we can find ways to share our world with wildlife.

Osprey — Jerry Eisner

Barn Owl — Todd Entrikin

Bald Eagle — Raymond Parsons

Northern Harrier — Phil Green

Red-tailed Hawk — Raymond Parsons

The Skagit and Samish Flats are fantastic for raptors because the grassy fields, especially fallow fields, support enormous quantities of voles which are eaten by many species of raptors. FACING PAGE: A Short-eared Owl swoops.

Eddie McHugh

Christine Kitch

Lee Mann

Steve Satushek

Fir Island, the delta of the Skagit River, bordered by the north and south forks, is home to agriculture, birds, salmon, and people, among other things. This sets up a complex, and at times conflictual, interaction of needs and desires in land use. However all share the goal of having a sound ecosystem and prosperous future.

ABOVE: Bales of local hay on the move. TOP RIGHT: A flock of Dunlin swish back and forth in a tight ball attempting to outmaneuver a falcon. RIGHT: A bird's-eye view of tilled fields.

Farming for Wildlife

Shorebirds and People Far into the Future

![Left to right, Gail Thulen, Colleen Thulen, Dave Hedlin, Serena Campbell, Vickie Mesman, Alan Mesman.]

Suzanne Fogarty

Left to right, Gail Thulen, Colleen Thulen, Dave Hedlin, Serena Campbell, Vickie Mesman, Alan Mesman.

When the Skagit Flats were marshes, they must have been an important feeding area for migrating shorebirds. Now, many species of shorebirds are in decline as a result of wetland habitat loss. In an attempt to replace some of the lost habitat and again make the valley a vital stop where shorebirds can feed and rest on their incredible journeys, The Nature Conservancy, in conjunction with Skagitonians to Preserve Farmland, Western Washington Agricultural Association, Washington State University, the Environmental Protection Agency, and three Skagit farmers are trying an experiment they call Farming for Wildlife.

Each of the three farmers, Alan Mesman, Dave Hedlin, and Gail Thulen, has leased about 70 acres of his farm land to be used in this experimental project to see if the land can be managed to provide

Christine Kitch

better shorebird habitat and improve the fertility of the land for farming. One field on each farm is flooded with a few inches of water, while a second is pastured, and a third is harvested monthly. Careful monitoring of the shorebirds throughout the project will provide a picture of which species feed on which areas, in what numbers, and at what tide cycle. The project will last for three years, and then the data will be analyzed. The farmers hope that the flooded fields will be more productive once the water is removed than they were before, and that the flooding will also kill agricultural pests. If flooding proves beneficial to both shorebirds and farmers, flooding may become a standard part of crop rotation and make the Skagit Delta a prosperous place for shorebirds and people far into the future.

—Howard Armstrong

Martin Burwash

Christine Kitch

Christine Kitch

Al Anderson

Pat Buller

Corwin Fergus

The Skagit Valley is home to many forms of agriculture. Over 90 different crops are grown in the county. Blueberries, raspberries, strawberries, tulips, daffodils, pickling cucumbers, specialty potatoes, Jonagold apples, green peas, and vegetable seed are some of the more important crops grown in this maritime valley.

CLAYTON JAMES, *Artist*

Clayton James in his La Conner art studio.

Andrew Szurek

Clayton James's art has an aching beauty to it. "People say that it makes them want to cry," once commented his late wife Barbara James.

Clayton has painted, made furniture, and sculpted in clay, wood, and concrete. Art critic Richard Campbell says "More than objects of art, James's ceramic pieces seem to represent a spirituality of place." For many, Clayton's paintings capture the quintessential image of the Skagit: reflections of diffused light and wild skies.

Clayton first came to the Northwest during WWII as a conscientious objector. Coming from the Midwest, he recalls being amazed by the powerful ocean and huge skunk cabbage. He remained in the Northwest and married Barbara, a talented artist herself, who eventually became the curator of the Museum of Northwest Art in La Conner. He and Barbara were part of an artistic era and community that saw the emergence of a distinctive Northwest style.

At 90, as Clayton paints in his shingled La Conner studio, inspired by the vistas and life surrounding him; it is evident that the need to make art still thrives in him. He not only paints the region's landscapes but is an ardent supporter of conservation. Fearful that our natural lands will be forever lost, he laments, "How are we going to turn this civilization around?" Yet, he says

this as he hands his guests vegetables from his extensive organic garden, indicating that sharing talent and food are two ways he has found to help make a difference.

"Life as an artist is pretty concentrated," he says. "Ceramic work was fine, but half of them exploded." As only one who creates for the love of creating could say, he adds, "I like the Native American theory—to work you have the right, but not to the fruits therein."

—*Molly Doran*

Yellow Night, Clayton James, 1961, Acrylic on canvas, 38.25 in. x 67 in., Collection of the Museum of Northwest Art, gift of Phyllis D. Massar.

Brett Baunton

Martin Burwash

Kirsten Morse

Wade Clark Jr.

Kelli Christoferson

72

John Sedgwick

La Conner is a small but bustling town, home to artists, full of tourists, and surrounded by fields of tulips and other crops. The annual Skagit Valley Tulip Festival in April brings traffic to a stand still and thousands of viewers to the valley. More tulip, iris, and daffodil bulbs are produced here than in any other county in the United States.

Jan Searle

LEFT: Brian Cladoosby's grandfather Henry Cladoosby fishes on Swinomish Slough. Photo: Ferd Brady, 1930. ABOVE: Brian Cladoosby wears a woven cedar bark hat.

BRIAN CLADOOSBY, *Tribal Chair, Swinomish Indian Tribal Community*

Can you talk about this place called Skagit and its importance to you, your family, and Coast Salish people?

When your roots go so deep in this area—we've been here so long—it's just a special place to live. We never had to be nomads. Everything that we needed to sustain ourselves has always been right here. The salmon was here twelve months out of the year; our elders just had to go down to the Swinomish Channel—in January, the steelhead would arrive; in April and May, the spring kings; in August, the pink salmon; in September, the silver salmon; in October and November, the chum salmon; and in December, the steelhead would return. In the summer the berries would ripen and the camas root would come out. We call it home, and we'll always call it home.

My grandfather's grandfather never saw a white man growing up. His name was Kelkahltsoot. He signed the Treaty for our tribe. That was not very long ago—four generations. I think about that time, what this place must have looked like, and what the Magic Skagit was like when he was growing up. Everything was pure, nothing was degraded. In 1855, when we signed the Treaty, the whole Skagit Valley was a nursery for millions upon millions of salmon. The river must have been a magnificent sight to see.

We always think in terms of seven generations. You want to make sure that what you leave for the seventh generation, is more or better than what you received. So when we think seven generations out, we have to think of those children that aren't born yet. I've got a granddaughter now, Isabella Bryanne, and she is the seventh generation from my grandfather's grandfather, Kelkahltsoot. It will

© Natalie Fobes, www.fobesphoto.com

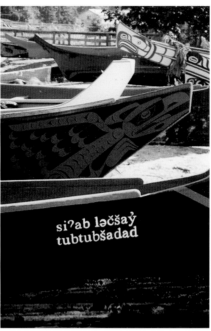

si?ab ləčšaỷ
tubtubšadad

Theresa Trebon, Swinomish Indian Tribal Community archive

LEFT: Catching salmon at Lone Tree Point. RIGHT: The Canoe Journey lands at Swinomish Indian Nation.

be her turn at some point to make sure that she takes care of the seventh generation coming behind her.

My first memory of being on the water with my family was right here on the Swinomish Channel. I must have been about three or four years old. I still get teased about it to this day because while Dad was laying out his net I fell asleep on it, and he grabbed me by my ankles and dunked me in the Channel to wake me up. Another special place is the mouth of the Skagit. I've been fishing for thirty years now and being able to work the mouth of the Skagit near Bald Island holds a special place in my heart.

Lone Tree Point is another special spot. Our elders have always run beach seine nets there. To be able to be out there at the end of summer with half a dozen families working together catching the salmon is special. Someday I will bring my granddaughter to Lone Tree, to Bald Island, and to the Channel to fish for salmon.

Salmon has always been a very sacred part of our culture. The Creator has given us one of the best river systems in the Salish Sea, and we thank him continually for supplying us with such magnificent food for our table. We've also been given a very big responsibility to manage the natural resources. We can't do it alone. It is very important that we create partnerships. Instead of pointing fingers and saying it's your fault that these resources have diminished or it's your fault these rivers aren't producing, we have to focus on solutions that work for all of us.

The Swinomish people have always been a people that have shared and cared for anyone that came into our area. We want to be thought of as good neighbors in this most sacred Skagit place we call home. Hopefully, we will have partners that will feel the same way we do and want to protect this special place for future generations.

—*Interview by Rusty Kuntze*

Shorelines & Bays

Like a Spoon in Soup

Carl Molesworth

Dick Smith

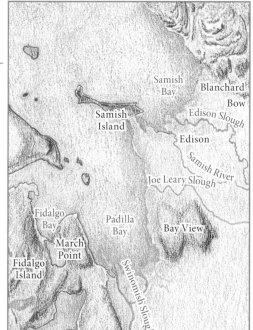

Full-size map on inside cover & page 1

From saltwater shorelines to open plains and high mountains, Skagit County boasts many of the elements of America in miniature. The west end of mainland Skagit County dips into Puget Sound like a spoon in soup. On the south side, the two forks of the Skagit River slide into Skagit Bay; on the north side, the Samish River enters Samish Bay; and between them is the glorious estuary of Padilla Bay.

Even a casual observer can't help noticing that the shores of all three bays are diked, forming hard boundaries between tidewaters and farmland that are as powerful symbolically and historically as they are structurally. Prior to the mid-1800s, several Coast Salish native tribes lived lightly on the Skagit coastline, gathering sustenance from the land, river, and sea. The arrival of Euro-American settlers changed all that. In 1863, they began diking low-lying salt marshes to convert them to farmland. By the turn of the 20th century, much of the lower Skagit Valley was encircled by the dikes we see today.

Measuring about eight miles long and three miles across, Padilla Bay is a natural treasure. The beach at Bay View State Park draws visitors to the bay from near and far to enjoy its views of sea, mountains, and sky. On the southern quarter stand the snow-capped Olympic Mountains; due west is the humpy green stretch of Fidalgo Island, with the March Point oil refineries in the foreground; and north, beyond the San Juan Islands, the bay drops off to the horizon as it meets the Strait of Georgia.

Phil Green

ABOVE: The tanks of Shell Puget Sound and Tesoro Corporation refineries on March Point in the foreground, with Mount Baker standing a majestic 10,781 feet high about 40 miles away. LEFT: The Red-winged Blackbird lives in wetlands and agricultural areas of coastal Skagit County. With its bright shoulder flashes and familiar "cherr" call, the male Red-winged Blackbird is quite a ladies' man, keeping track of up to 15 different females making nests in his territory.

But the view is just one quality of many that makes Padilla Bay a special place—special enough to be among just 27 such bodies in the United States designated a National Estuarine Research Reserve (NERR). A place where fresh water fed by sloughs draining Bay View hill and the surrounding farmland meets the salt water of the Puget Sound-Georgia Basin, intertidal Padilla Bay is a veritable mixing bowl of life. It is flooded at high tide, but when the tide goes out the whole bay empties, exposing miles of mud flats. This condition allows unusually large eelgrass meadows to grow.

In fact, Padilla Bay has about 8,000 acres of eelgrass, which makes it the largest contiguous eelgrass bed found between

Todd Entrikin

The eelgrass beds of Skagit County are essential habitat for a variety of creatures, from the brooding anemone living on the grass blades and hooded nudibranchs capturing small crustaceans (inset) to mating Dungeness crabs (above).

Photos: Jim Ramaglia

Southern California and Alaska, hence the large number of brant that visit every year. Eelgrass serves as a nursery for salmon, crab, perch, and herring. It also is home to worms, shrimp, clams, and other invertebrates that, in turn, are food for Great Blue Herons, eagles, otters, seals, and humans. That's why Padilla Bay was set aside in 1980 for research and education about Puget Sound.

Before 1980, however, the future of Padilla Bay was anything but certain. The vast mud flats so valuable as eelgrass habitat also drew the attention of people who had other ideas in mind. An early plan was to push the dikes westward all the way to the

Swinomish Channel and drain the bay so it could be used for farmland. Another plan emerged in the mid-20th century to fill the bay, Venice-like, and build houses on it, each home having a parking space for a boat out front. Yet another plan would have had the bay converted into an industrial park.

Due to historic subdivision of tidelands, the ownership of Padilla Bay was in private hands and highly fragmented, with 1,789 separate parcels. Would-be developers were serious and bought up large portions of the bay. But strong opposition existed among the people who lived in the neighboring area. The voice

Christine Kitch

Thomas Plank

Ric Merry

John Scurlock

TOP LEFT AND RIGHT: The Samish River Delta hosts abundant shellfish and bird populations. BOTTOM LEFT: Padilla Bay at low tide. BOTTOM RIGHT: Skagit Land Trust's work with the Texaco Trustees Restoration Committee and the Washington Department of Natural Resources (DNR) to return tidelands to public ownership in south Fidalgo Bay for the benefit of future generations has been hugely successful—532 acres of tidelands are now owned by DNR and protected with a conservation easement held by Skagit Land Trust.

Educational programs at the Padilla Bay National Estuarine Research Reserve connect local school children to nature with activities that teach them about the fragile ecology of Skagit County's shorelines and the efforts under way to protect them. RIGHT: All photos taken at Padilla Bay.

Brenda Cunningham

Lauren Foster decides where to dig.

of retired teacher Edna Breazeale, whose family operated a dairy farm on the shore of Padilla Bay in Bay View, stood out.

"We'd all grown up in the area and had enjoyed being children here," Edna later told an interviewer. "We wanted it kept this way so others could enjoy it. So many places are closed now. There are signs everywhere saying keep off the beach, keep off this and that. But there should be places where children can see how things grow naturally."

Edna helped organize a grassroots resistance, lobbying the Washington State Legislature and gathering signatures on petitions. It's an early—and stunning—local example of the power of activism. By 1974, state and federal working groups were trying to identify areas in Washington that would be eligible for Estuarine Reserve status under the new Coastal Zone Management Act. Padilla Bay eventually was selected due to its unique physical and biological qualities. It didn't hurt that Edna Breazeale had willed her family's farm to the state for use as the site of an interpretive center. The Governor's Padilla Bay Sanctuary Steering Committee and Technical Advisory Subcommittee established the original proposed boundary for the Padilla Bay NERR in 1979, and the federal designation came the following year.

The Washington State Department of Ecology is responsible for the administration and management of the Padilla Bay Reserve. The original major private owner of tidelands, the Orion

aritza Chavez reviews samples.   Franco DeLao showing collection tray.   Susan Wood, the Estuary Soup Chef.

Corp., settled an 11-year litigation effort with the state in 1993, and its 8,004 acres were transferred to the Department of Ecology for $3.6 million. Over the years, the Reserve has purchased other properties within the boundary as they became available.

Today, the shorelines of Skagit County are the subject of intense research and effort as scientists and activists seek to protect their rich diversity of life forms, from the Great Blue Herons of March Point to the five runs of Skagit salmon, the shellfish beds in Samish Bay, and much more. This work is the dike that holds back threats to the shorelines such as pollution and invasive species. And, like the Skagit dikes, this work must not fail.

Padilla Bay National Estuarine Research Reserve

Edna Breazeale, who played a major role in the establishment of the Padilla Bay National Estuarine Research Reserve, speaks in 1982 at the grand opening of the center that bears her family's name.

Phil Green

ABOVE: A Belted Kingfisher lives up to its name, flying off with a fingerling it has just plucked in its long beak. The shoreline of Skagit County is renowned for the variety and number of birds that live there, attracting many thousands of binocular-wielding visitors every year.

LEFT: Padilla Bay is among just 27 bodies of water in the United States protected from development by its designation as a National Estuarine Research Reserve.

Phil Green

At low tide, the shorelines and bays of Skagit County reveal all sorts of natural treasure, such as the long stalks of bull kelp and fragments of rockweed, which look like small green mittens, seen here. Many organisms take refuge under these mats of seaweed to conserve moisture.

FACING PAGE, BOTTOM (from left to right): An eel-like gunnel fish hides amongst an abundant diversity of sponges, corals, and sea squirts; a beautiful Christmas anemone unfolds its stinging tentacles like a flower, as a small kelp crab passes by; an elegant blood star seems to be running across the sponge encrusted rocks.

Christine Kitch

Kirsten Morse

Olympia
Oyster, Taylor
Shellfish Farms

ABOVE: The waters of Samish Bay nurture several commercial oyster-growing operations. The oyster beds are laid out in geometric patterns that promote efficiency and are easy to spot from the air. ABOVE RIGHT: A clam digger, with obligatory rake and bucket, makes his way along a Skagit County beach. Clam digging is a popular sport among those with a taste for the meaty bivalve mollusks.

Jim Ramaglia

Phil Green

Jim Ramaglia

87

Mankind has left its mark on the shoreline areas in concrete and steel. The Duane Berentson Bridge on Highway 20 (above left) connects the mainland with Fidalgo Island; Refineries on March Point (below) have been producing petroleum products for half a century.

Settlers began building dikes in the 1860s so they could convert low-lying salt marshes to farmland.
ABOVE: Men digging a drainage ditch on the Samish Flats north of Edison, District #18, 1910. Back row, left to right: Bovitz Omdal, Roy Brown, unidentified, Henry Abel, John Haaland, Jim Taylor, Roscoe Taylor. Standing on the bank are Ingvalf Larson, Pete Hansen, John Taylor, and Mr. Tucker.

Brenda Cunningham   Brenda Cunningham   Phil Green

The March Point Heronry, the main portion of which is a Skagit Land Trust conservation area, is home to nearly 600 Great Blue Heron nests. ABOVE LEFT: A technician performs maintenance of the Heron Webcam, which helps scientists and the general public keep an eye on the big birds and their chicks. The Heron Webcam can be seen by visiting the Padilla Bay website from March through August, *www.padillabay.gov/education_heron.html.*

In 1994, Bud and Vera Kinney donated 3.5 acres on March Point to Skagit Land Trust. The forested property was already home to more than 100 Great Blue Heron nests, and the Kinneys wanted to see the area protected.

Great Blue Herons have nested on this property since the late 1970s. In recent years it has become apparent that this nesting site plays a significant role in maintaining the heron population of the greater Puget Sound area. In 1984, 42 nests were counted at this site, with a steady increase ever since. By 2003, March Point Heronry boasted nearly 600 nests.

Although the number of heron nests at March Point has increased dramatically, the heron population of the area has not.

"There is a growing concern that small heronries throughout Skagit County are being abandoned because of encroaching development and the herons are congregating in fewer locations, making protection of these nesting locations all the more critical," says Skagit Land Trust executive director Molly Doran. Loss of foraging habitat elsewhere may also be drawing the birds to March Point.

—*Carl Molesworth*

Brenda Cunningham

March Point Heronry

89

Samish Indian Nation

Growing Stronger Together

Brenda Cunningham

The Samish Canoe Family received 75 baby cedar trees from the Potlatch Fund for youth and visitors to restore salmon habitats along the Canoe Journey route, learning the importance of our relationships with the environment and each other in the process.

"Why should baby cedar trees be planted close together?" Inter-tribal youth visiting the Samish Nation for the Canoe Journey were asked to guess the answer before getting into pairs and planting their baby cedar trees in an Environmental Awareness Project.

"Because they lean on each other and grow strong together" was the correct answer, and a number of their responses were close, "So the wind doesn't knock them over." "So they can shade each other." And a response that drew applause from on-looking adults, "Because they love each other."

Samish Indian Nation historical archives

Nicole Herman

Nicole Herman

ABOVE LEFT: Samish Indians, led by Hul-hot-ten (Harry Samish), sail along the shore of Samish Island, late 1800s. CENTER: The traveling canoes help to carry the culture of Samish ancestors to tribal members reminding them of their interdependence with one another, Mother Earth, and the waves that connect us all. RIGHT: Tribal Chairman Tom Wooten welcomes incoming canoes as paddlers complete the Samish leg of the Canoe Journey.

In much the same way as young cedar trees support and protect each other, tribal canoe families traveling mainly in cedar canoes rely on one another throughout the Canoe Journeys each summer, for safety, comfort, and companionship. When one canoe family is low on energy and lagging behind, another canoe family will slow down and sing songs to them to lift their spirits, or share some food and water if needed. Why do you usually see canoes traveling in pairs along the Journey? It comes down to a simple yet profound answer, "because they love each other."

—*Leslie Eastwood, General Manager, Samish Indian Nation*

The Samish River is a separate drainage from the Skagit, flowing out of the Cascade foothills east of Lake Whatcom and through the fertile valley floor outside Burlington to dump into Samish Bay near the community of Edison.

Life in the Samish Basin is a laid-back affair. Artists and musicians rub elbows with farmers and fishermen, while resident dogs sleep in the streets of Edison with little risk to themselves or anyone else.

And always there is the scenery. In any season, fair weather or foul, the Samish Basin delights residents and visitors alike with its sweeping vistas and intimate vignettes.

Thomas Plank

Geoff Peterson

Geoff Peterson

Therese Ogle

The Islands

Stepping Stones to the Sea

Jan Hersey

Phil Green

6.

N

Full-size map on inside cover & page 1

The forks, sloughs, rivulets, and creeks of the Skagit River separate the valley floor into ever more isolated, increasingly rugged fragments until, at last, huge chunks stand, literally, like stepping stones to the Salish Sea.

In fact, these islands, like all of the San Juan Archipelago of which they're a part, are the geologic stragglers, slipping eastward at a fir-pitch pace to one day unite with the mainland. Carried by plate tectonics, tipped like an up-ended lasagna, and scoured by glaciers, the islands that comprise Skagit County's western boundary reveal a rare glimpse of the layers of the Earth's mantle, once buried beneath an ancient sea. Now craggy amalgams of multi-layered rocks covered with a skim coat of soil, they are the fragile shoreline intersection of earth and ocean, an essential, if increasingly threatened, link in our interconnected web.

The Island Family

Fidalgo, Guemes, Cypress, Sinclair. Hat, Saddlebag, Cone, Jack . . . some two dozen small islands float like gulls in the salty sea of Skagit's raggedy edge, their names the remnants of a cultural ragout of passing natives, explorers, and immigrants.

Rippled highways and bridges keep islanders connected. LEFT: Guemes Island is worlds apart, and a five-minute ferry ride across Guemes Channel from downtown Anacortes (seen in the background). TOP RIGHT: Deception Pass Bridge, completed in 1935, connects Fidalgo and Whidbey Islands, 180 feet above churning eight-knot currents. BOTTOM RIGHT: Washington State Ferries, along with a full complement of working and pleasure boats, connect Fidalgo Island and the mainland with the San Juan Islands and British Columbia's Vancouver Island.

Anacortes, the islands' lone incorporated town with some 16,400 residents, anchors Fidalgo, the largest and most populated island. Nearby Guemes Island hosts permanent residents and part-timers, often passionate advocates for their laid back, rural lifestyle.

Located "off the grid," Cypress and Sinclair shelter small numbers of resourceful summer and fulltime residents. But the majority of Skagit's islands remain unpopulated, either too small, inaccessible, or mere rocky outcroppings.

Island Magnetism

Despite natural assaults from wind, sun, water, and the mounting pressures of human presence, the islands have long been treasured for their breath-halting beauty and natural

Sandy Carter

Phil Green

For visitors and residents alike, Skagit County island waters are a world-class, year-round playground. LEFT: As seen from Cypress Island, a fire-lit sunset illuminates Mt. Baker and the Sisters Range on the mainland.

TOP RIGHT: Locally built Nordic Tugs at anchor in Anacortes's Skyline Marina. BOTTOM RIGHT: Fortunate whale watchers might happen upon a spy-hopping orca whale, recently added to the federal Endangered Species list.

《 Brett Baunton

103

Steve Berentson

LEFT: Citywide events bring out locals and visitors to share the fun of island living. Each September, laid back Anacortes heats up with the arrival of the Oyster Run and hundreds of spangly Harleys, their leather-clad handlers and, of course, fresh oysters.

BOTTOM LEFT: Between 1920 and 1926, community members, directed by architect John LePage, built Anacortes's folk art style Causland Park to honor servicemen who died in WWI. Mosaic walls, decorative elements, and an amphitheater are fashioned from thousands of native rocks in varying hues.

BOTTOM CENTER: Everyone gets in on boat building during the Anacortes Waterfront Festival, held each May.

BOTTOM RIGHT: Kids join in Fourth of July fun on Guemes Island with an old-fashioned hayride in the sunshine.

Steve Berentson

Jan Hersey

Thea LaCross

PHILIP MCCRACKEN, *Artist*

Guemes Island's rural patchwork of farms, forests, and beaches is central to the art and life of Philip McCracken, an eminent American sculptor and third-generation Skagitonian. Not only does Phil coax emotion and affection from the island's natural forms, he finds a comforting organic wholeness in its independent, close-knit community.

"I feel a powerful sense of place here," says Phil, who has lived on Guemes with his wife Anne for over 50 years. "The land, the creatures—Nature is kind here."

With an art degree from the University of Washington, in 1954 Phil sought an apprenticeship in London with innovative British sculptor, Henry Moore. Says Phil, "Moore was the artist I admired most, but he was also a family man. Art and family, that's what I wanted for myself from the beginning." As luck would have it, Phil met Anne MacFetridge while sailing to England. The two were married six weeks later. Moore was their best man.

As Moore's daughter Mary had been a frequent studio visitor in London, the McCrackens' three sons were welcome in Phil's Guemes studio, as were neighborhood children, apprentices, and "fellow travelers," including a skunk, deer, monkey, and Great Horned Owl that amicably shared the McCracken home. Connections Phil forged with these critters, and while roaming and rowing Skagit's woodlands and islands, find expression through his sculpture, drawings, and paintings—abalone shell arcing into bird song; the lowly potato bearing earth's wisdom; polygons carved from the night sky.

Suzanne Fogarty

Dick Garvey

Completed in 2001, Guemes Island Totem (right), bronze, 23¼ inches, is one of the artist's favorite sculptures and an homage to the many "fellow travelers" who share his path.

"Phil's art is about essence," says his wife Anne. Adds a friend, "Philip takes the object, sees all the details, and then he takes them all away . . . and gives you back your imagination."

Phil, himself, is reluctant to intellectualize his work's inspiration or pigeonhole its meaning. "Influences are everywhere," he says. "I simply stay open to them. What's yours will stick, others will fall away."

—*Jan Hersey*

GEORGE FAHEY
Grandfather & Land Steward

In 1930, when George Fahey was just 19, he drove with his mother from Seattle to Skagit County, waiting anxiously on the courthouse steps alongside a handful of land auction bidders. With limited money in his pocket, he knew that if anyone else bid on the parcel he'd come for, he'd walk away with a broken heart.

No one else came that spring morning to purchase the land George had fallen in love with as a kid. His $50 cash down payment secured an old farm, woods, and tidelands at Tide Point, on remote Cypress Island—nearly 100 acres that have since anchored three generations of his family.

Cypress is a magical place, as early tribes, a few 1890s hardscrabble homesteaders, and recent conservationists attest. Remaining mostly untouched, it is the largest undeveloped island of the San Juans, without ferry service, paved roads, or utilities. Timber has been cut over time, but today, sunlight slants through 100-year-old second growth onto old logging roads that wind through densely packed salal and sword ferns, passing streams, wetlands, and secluded lakes. Raven and flicker calls pierce the island hush. Coves, rocky beaches, and sandy bluffs trace a convoluted shoreline. Limited trails allow public exploration and panoramic views from Eagle Rock, home to protected nesting raptors.

Preservation has not always been easy. In the 1960s, a coalition of Cypress advocates successfully stifled developers' efforts to

Suzanne Fogarty

LEFT: Three generations of the Fahey family—patriarch George, son Nick, and granddaughter Anna—gather to celebrate the decision to place a conservation easement on the family's 99-acre Cypress Island (in background) property with Skagit Land Trust.

Christine Kitch

Tide Point, the Fahey family's Cypress Island property.

blanket the island with a 4,000-acre, five-star resort. Today, only 450 of Cypress's 5,500 acres are privately owned; the rest was acquired over time by the Washington Department of Natural Resources as one of its first Natural Resources Conservation Areas and recently an Aquatic Reserve.

In January 2008, the Faheys quietly made their own contribution. Near the courthouse steps where he first anxiously waited, 97-year-old George Fahey, his son Nick, and his grandchildren, Anna and Joe, signed a conservation easement with Skagit Land Trust on their Tide Point property—yet another sort of down payment, one that continues the family's stewardship and preserves a valuable piece of the island's magic in perpetuity.

—*Anna Fahey and Jan Hersey*

Skagit County's island edges draw people out of doors year round. Whether examining beach critters, hiking the periphery of Anacortes's 220-acre Washington Park (right), or exploring the working waterfront by kayak (bottom right). The *Veteran* (bottom left), a 1926 purse seiner restored by Nick Fahey, is typical of those that have fished for salmon in the Pacific Northwest since the early 1900s.

Andrew Cline

Steve Berentson

Neil Rabinowitz

Thomas Plank

Steve Satushek

Jan Hersey

Jan Hersey

Sunlight pierces woodland and kelp forests (above and facing page), revealing the layers of life required to support our fragile interconnected web. LEFT: In the forest, salal and thimbleberry seek out light near the forest's edge. FACING PAGE: A recreational diver explores the rocky bottom, swimming over bull kelp and a field of plumose anemones. CENTER: A juvenile rockfish, and right, a fireworks-like, white-and-orange-tipped nudibranch.

Jim Ramaglia

Kelley Scarzafava

Phil Green

Phil Green

109

Phil Green

Phil Gree

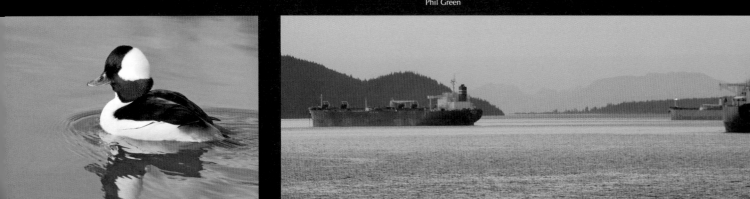

Margaret Saint Clair

Todd Entrikir

Marine life, oil, and jobs share a fragile dependency on Pacific Northwest waters. CLOCKWISE FROM UPPER LEFT: A river otter enjoys a tasty meal of crab on the rocks. Red-billed Oyster Catchers ply the shoreline using their chisel-like bills to pry open mussels and other shellfish. In Fidalgo Bay, oil tankers wait to load and unload at the Tesoro and Shell refineries. With its white head patch and small gray bill, the boldly marked Bufflehead adapts to fresh- and saltwater bodies of all sizes.

FACING PAGE: Washington Park's iconic juniper is silhouetted against a pastel sunset above Burrows Channel, with Burrows and Lopez Islands and the Olympic Peninsula beyond.

Lee Mann

Leaving a Natural Legacy

Bill Dietrich

So here we are in God's pocket, Eden with big-box stores and clearcuts, stupefied by our good fortune and scared to death we're going to pave paradise and be cast out of the Garden. We're dazzled, daily, by our more than two dozen major Skagit Islands, Shire-like farmland, muscular rivers, mist-softened forests, and glaciered peaks.

Wow! Unbelievable! We're here! Skagit County is changing! So what do we do now? Let's take the long view.

It took 13.73 billion years to make this place. That's how long astronomers think the Universe has been perking along to turn primordial hydrogen and helium into the atoms of heavier elements that make up everything we see today. Stars had to be born, burn, explode, and coalesce into new solar systems to make the atoms of where we live and who we are.

Star leftovers—not a bad thing to be.

Then 4.5 billion years for our own planet to cool and spin into its present configuration, half a billion years of development toward higher organisms, and millions of years to accrete Skagit County onto North America from floating dibs and dabs of rock that docked to extend the continent westward. As a finishing touch, the last 13,000 years turned what must have been pretty much a gravel pit, after the recent Ice Age, into the costly real estate we see today.

By geological standards, our farmland is fresh as new carpet, our vistas the blink of an eye.

Native Americans have probably been here for at least 10,000 years. Then the pioneers. And then? A sleepy stasis—still in living memory—that even today influences the way some Skagitonians view our home as placid, protected backwater. From 1910 to 1970, Skagit County gained only 23,000 people. The valley seemed timeless.

Then, boom! Someone punched the accelerator. In the next 30 years, Skagit County's population nearly doubled, to 102,979 in 2000. It is approximately 117,500 as this book is published, if state projections are correct. The mid-range state prediction is that there will be 178,036 of us by 2030, just one generation away.

That's an average of nearly 3,000 more people in each of the next 22 years, or the need to build—in one generation—another Mount Vernon, Anacortes, Burlington, and Sedro Woolley.

Tim Chandonnet

Chuckanut sandstone meets the sea.

The good news is that Skagit County, which averages 59 people for each of its 1,735 square miles, is still below the average United States density of 79.6. We live in a place not-yet-too-crowded, with so much potential that the best marriage of human and wild is yet to come.

The bad news is that we're packed mostly into the relatively small river valley and delta that is easily developable. Every land-use decision we make is important because we mostly live on top of each other. About half of Skagit County is public land. Just three percent of the county is in urban growth areas, and eight percent is classified as "rural" under the comprehensive plan. Much of the rest is industrial timber land and agricultural lands.

What has become vital, then, are the riverbanks, shorelines, wetlands, creek watersheds, pocket woodlands, pastures, and farms that are right next to people. That's what creates our breathtaking mosaic. And that's what is mostly unprotected and could be lost: Snow Geese and potato trucks, grazing elk and performing arts centers, storm-lashed tidepools and tulip-field Victorian houses.

Humans are part of our landscape, and (by rumor, at least) there are some out there who think the recent growth is the best thing that ever happened to Skagit County. They can't wait for more. Bring it on! Egads.

Assuming that the rest of us, however, live here because we don't want to live in Orange County, what do we do to keep Skagit, Skagit?

Which brings us to the point of this book. What you can do is help Skagit Land Trust and the 27 conservation organizations it partners with to conserve and protect the most important and threatened land in Skagit County. It's a voluntary, cost-effective, non-partisan, non-regulatory program of unity and partnership. And it works. Achieve immortality. Help leave a patch of green, forever. Skagit Land Trust makes it so easy!

It was in 1992, after a decade in which Skagit grew by 15,000 people and was about (in the next decade) to grow by 20,000 more, that three Audubon Society members recognized the need for a new, non-profit, volunteer organization. It would encourage and administer conservation easements to protect precious natural areas.

Their names are Harold Christenson, Keith Wiggers, and Gene Murphy, and they planted the proverbial acorn that is growing into an oak. Relying on donations and the incredible goodwill of property owners, Skagit Land Trust has gone from

Suzanne Fogarty

Harold Christenson, Keith Wiggers, and Gene Murphy founded Skagit Land Trust in 1992.

assets of $5,000 its first year to $5 million today, and from 32 charter members to 670 households and businesses.

In just 16 years, Skagit Land Trust has achieved permanent protection of 5,500 acres and 24 miles of river, lake, and saltwater shoreline. "Our mission is saving land for tomorrow," says Molly Doran, the Trust's executive director.

Saving, not locking up. The Trust works to provide public access when feasible. One notable example is the late physician and climber Fred Darvill, who built a trail so others could enjoy the permanent protection of his property. "He wanted this place to be the way it was when he fell in love with it," said his wife, Ginny Darvill. And it is.

The middle Skagit River is slowly returning to the natural conditions that once supported great salmon runs. The region's largest heronry has been protected. Anacortes forest lands have moved from timber resource to permanent park. Hurn Field has become an elk grazing area that is a new tourist stop on Highway 20. There is poetry in the roll of places already saved. Elysium Meadows, Cumberland Creek, the Keller-Karlberg Cascade, and Butler Flats. Big Rock, Little Mountain, Mud Lake, and Diobsud Creek.

Nookachamps, Suiattle, and Kosbab Slough. And those are just a few examples.

When a family like the Faheys puts an easement on nearly a hundred acres of Cypress Island that would make a developer drool, you know something remarkable is going on.

Painful compromise is being forged on Blanchard Mountain. The Chuckanut Highlands have the potential to be one of the finest and most important green corridors and ecological highways on Interstate 5. Land has been protected on Barney Lake, Minkler Lake, and Lake Campbell. This is stuff future generations will marvel at.

All of this happened through partnerships. Agencies like the U.S. Forest Service and Washington State Department of Natural Resources, organizations like Skagit Land Trust, The Nature Conservancy, Ducks Unlimited, Skagit Watershed Council, Skagit Fisheries Enhancement Group, and professionals like realtors and lawyers have partnered to pull off deal after amazing deal. For once we're not too late. We're acting before Eden is overrun—and doing such a good job at keeping this place beautiful that it will make more valuable the places where we do live.

Careful conservation is smart investment.

The sun's morning rays shine through the trees.

Wade Clark Jr.

So here's what you can do. The fortunate few who own large parcels of land can consider placing a conservation easement on all or a portion of their land. This is a flexible agreement—the owner gets to negotiate the terms, in detail—that limit future development and protects the natural land.

They may qualify for a tax break to reflect the loss of potential value from giving up the development rights of the property. That means you can save Eden and get paid for it, sort of. Of course, the devil is in the details, and that's why Skagit Land Trust and other groups like Skagitonians to Preserve Farmland, Skagit County Farmland Legacy Program, and San Juan Preservation Trust have expert staffs to advise you on your options.

You leave the best kind of monument to yourself: natural beauty that will be appreciated for generations to come. If you're not a large landowner, you can help by giving money. Your donations help pay for that expert staff or sometimes to help pay for outright acquisition of key properties: Skagit Land Trust has 16 of them now. Anything helps. Start, for example, by buying and giving away another copy of this book. Every word and picture in it was donated for free; every dollar of profit goes to the Trust for land conservation.

Community volunteers in action.

Do the donations work? You betcha. Collectively, land trusts nationwide have saved more land than is contained in the nation's lower 48 National Park System. If you've got more time than cash, then volunteer. Skagit Land Trust loves to put idealism to work. You can plant trees, clean up Trust lands, build improvements, serve as stewards who look after pieces of property, raise money, organize events, serve on the board, or tell your friends.

There are indirect ways to help the Trust and Skagit County as well. The simplest and most effective is to live as lightly as you can. Try to choose the more energy-efficient appliance. The higher-mileage vehicle. The improved level of insulation. Native plants over exotics that require too many pesticides and fertilizers. Recycle. Conserve. Combine errands. Walk. Bike. Think.

Most of the things that are good for the environment also save money and time, and are good for your health. The right thing is the smart thing is the cheap thing.

Become a "locavore." That's an oddball new word for people who buy produce and meat grown locally. It saves the fossil fuel needed for shipping and provides farmers with more income, making it easier for them to keep farming and resist development.

Speak up for Mother Nature by getting involved. This doesn't mean you have to run for office, join a party, enlist in a group, or subscribe to an ideology. Just let your elected officials or public servants or local news organizations know that the quality of life in Skagit County is important to you, and that not every good can be measured narrowly in dollars and cents.

Finally, fall in love all over again.

Fall in love with Skagit County.

When you live in a place, it's easy to take it for granted or not notice the gradual, insidious changes gnawing away at heaven. When you see every other pretty place overrun with uninspired development, it's easy to be resigned to the same happening here.

Jerry Haegele

Pete Haase

Skagit Land Trust

Fidalgo Fly Fishers

Tim Manns

Growth is inevitable. You can't stop progress. That's the best we can do. It's supposed to be ugly. I'm not in charge. What the heck, I'm almost dead.

Balderdash! The human race makes places as variant as Venice and Calcutta, Bhutan and Chernobyl, Napa and Houston, Carmel and Cleveland. We choose all the time between beautiful and utilitarian, innovative and ordinary, investment and cheap, smart and mindless, backwards and forwards, planned and sprawling, crowded and measured, paradise and purgatory.

Sometimes, it's the wrong people who are making the choices. Speak up!

We Americans love to "escape" on vacation, and "start over" with a move to someplace better. But that someplace is this place. Nobody is going to rescue us from ourselves, or tell us how to fix it, or forge compromises for us. We're the

Steve Philbrick

keepers of this particular garden, and generations unborn are going to be looking over their shoulders to see how we did.

Well, one thing we've done is start Skagit Land Trust. So if you're inspired at all by the words and pictures in this book, lend a hand. Individually, there's only so much we can do. But together we can make a difference—look at what Skagit Land Trust has accomplished in just 16 years!—and pass on to our children's children's children the same incredible array of gorgeous ecosystems that have infused, enlightened, and inspired our own lives.

Let's make it another 13.73 billion years.

By starting with what we can do today.

Bill Dietrich is a former Skagit Land Trust board member and Pulitzer Prize-winning journalist, university professor, and author of eleven books. His novels have been translated into 27 languages.

117

Skagit Land Trust protects wildlife habitat, wetlands, agriculture and forest lands, scenic open spaces, and shorelines throughout the mainland and islands of Skagit County for the benefit of our community and as a legacy for future generations.

Ric Merry

The Magic Skagit

"...it's there that agriculture, art and wild nature commingle in an unprecedented mix."

—Tom Robbins

"I feel a powerful sense of place here. The land, the creatures—Nature is kind here."

—Philip McCracken

"We're acting before Eden is overrun—and doing such a good job at keeping this place beautiful that it will make more valuable the places where we do live."

—Bill Dietrich

« Lee Mann

Project Manager and Creative Director

Patricia Chambers considers herself fortunate to have collaborated with such a talented group of people in helping to make this book. As the youngest member of a 12-sibling family, she learned the merits of teamwork and achieving consensus at an early age and is convinced that it was her destiny to be a part of this creative, collaborative adventure. Patricia has worked on publications for over 15 years as a graphic designer, editor, and writer and operates ECANDO Communications + Design, *www.ecando.org*. She lives in Bellingham, Washington with her husband Mark and their very brown dog Molly Brown.

Natural Skagit: A Journey from Mountains to Sea
published by Skagit Land Trust

Introduction by Tom Robbins
Epilogue by Bill Dietrich

Project Manager & Creative Director: Patricia Chambers

Edited and produced by Skagit Land Trust

Project Director: Renata Hoyle Maybruck

Editors: Patricia Chambers, Molly Doran

Copy Editor: Susan Witter

Proofreaders: Ron Feld, James Hoyle, Karen Krub, Susan Magorien

Fact Checker: Tim Manns

Layout & Design: Patricia Chambers

Photo Prepress: Brett Baunton, ArtScan.com

Portrait Photography: Suzanne Fogarty

Cartography: Brenda Cunningham (base map), Patricia Chambers (graphics)

Printed by Premier Graphics, Bellingham, WA.

Writers: Howard Armstrong, Patricia Chambers, Molly Doran, Leslie Eastwood, Anna Fahey, Jan Hersey, AJ "Rusty" Kuntze, Tim Manns, Libby Mills, Carl Molesworth, Megan Scott O'Bryan, Craig Romano, Theresa Trebon

Suzanne Fogarty

Steering Committee (from left to right): Carl Molesworth, Jan Hersey, Megan Scott O'Bryan, Renata Hoyle Maybruck, Ron Feld, Craig Romano, Howard Armstrong, Patricia Chambers, Libby Mills, Molly Doran.

Steering Committee

Howard Armstrong, a charter member of Skagit Land Trust, field trip leader, and past president of Skagit Audubon, has lived in Skagit County for over 40 years.

Molly Doran is the Executive Director of Skagit Land Trust. She and her husband Andrew Cline feel fortunate to be raising their two sons close to nature in the Skagit.

Ron Feld is a Skagit Land Trust Board member. He has been a practicing RN since 1982 and a certified mediator since 1991. He has been married since 1982 and a Skagitonian since 1995.

When not distracted by fly-by eagles and drive-by tugs, **Jan Hersey** writes about design, the environment, and the world in between from an office atop her garage, over looking Burrows Bay in Anacortes.

Renata Hoyle Maybruck (Project Director) is a sixth generation Skagitonian and Development and Communications Director for Skagit Land Trust. She enjoys gardening, traveling, and spending time with her husband Darren and son Dante at their home in Clear Lake.

Libby Mills is a field naturalist and birder who has studied Skagit Valley eagles since 1982 and enjoys teaching, photography, and field sketching from the Cascades to Padilla Bay.

A resident of Bay View, **Carl Molesworth** has been an editor and writer for 35 years. He currently edits two trade magazines and writes aviation history books.

Megan Scott O'Bryan is a realtor with Windermere Real Estate. She is the former manager of the family-owned Scott's Bookstore and is past president of the Pacific Northwest Bookseller's Association. She lives with her husband Matt and sons Will and Thomas in Mount Vernon.

Suzanne Fogarty

Brenda Cunningham

Photo Committee (from left to right): Steve Philbrick, Renata Hoyle Maybruck, Jerry Eisner, Lee Mann, Patricia Chambers, Keith Wiggers, Phil Green.

Craig Romano is an outdoors writer, co-creator of Hikeoftheweek.com and author of five books including *Day Hiking North Cascades* (Mountaineers Books). An avid hiker, runner, and paddler, he lives with his wife Heather and cat Giuseppe in Mount Vernon.

Photo Committee

Jerry Eisner is a local physician, who has enjoyed photography since age 5. Currently, his interest is digiscoping, which employs a camera attached to an astronomical telescope. His bird images utilize this technique.

Phil Green works for The Nature Conservancy as their Yellow Island Steward and previously coordinated Bald

Eagle studies on the Skagit and Sauk rivers. He is a former mathematics instructor at Skagit Valley College.

Lee Mann is a third generation Washingtonian and nature photographer who has been photographing landscapes and wildlife for over 35 years. His images are shown all over the world. He lives in Sedro-Woolley with his wife Ann and operates his photography business and studio with his son Bryce.

Steve Philbrick has lived in the Northwest and Skagit all of his life. He has a special appreciation for the ruggedness and delicate beauty of the people and landscape where "our civilization meets the primitive world."

Keith Wiggers is one of the founders of Skagit Land Trust and a retired veterinarian. He and his wife Jan have had life-long interests in the world's wildlife and habitats, and share their wildlife experiences through videography.

Special Contributors

Suzanne Fogarty is a wedding and portrait photographer based in Anacortes, where she resides with her two beautiful children. She never met an olive or a camera she didn't like, and thrives on every new inspiration that her clients, just by being who they are, bring her. *www.suzannefogarty.com*

AJ "Rusty" Kuntze is a Skagit Land Trust Board member and Chair of the Public Policy Committee. He worked for the Swinomish Tribe for 24 years as an attorney, tribal court administrator, and chief judge.

Special thanks to:
Bob Keller, editor of *Whatcom Places*, for inspiration and support.

Lee Mann for use of his professional photography studio for the photo jury process.

The photographers, steering and photo committee members, and volunteers who gave over 2,000 hours to this project, and Skagit Land Trust's supporters who make the Trust's conservation work possible.

Nancy Wagner

Index

Dave Smith

Natural Skagit: A Journey from Mountains to Sea
©2008 by Skagit Land Trust
All rights reserved
First edition, 2008
No part of this book may be reproduced in any form without permission
in writing from the publisher.

Published by Skagit Land Trust
P.O. Box 1017, Mount Vernon, WA 98273
(360) 428-7878
www.skagitlandtrust.org

Printed by Premier Graphics, Bellingham, WA

ISBN (Hardcover): 978-0-9821399-0-5
ISBN (Softcover): 978-0-9821399-1-2

Library of Congress Control Number: 2008908636

Lee Mann

SINCE 1992, Skagit Land Trust has been protecting wildlife habitat, wetlands, agriculture and forest lands, scenic open spaces, and shorelines throughout the mainland and islands of Skagit County for the benefit of our community and as a legacy for future generations. The Trust conserves the natural environment by purchasing properties; by helping other groups protect critical land; and through permanent protection agreements, called conservation easements, with private and public landowners. Once land is protected, staff and volunteers restore and maintain the Trust's conservation areas. The public is invited to view wildlife at several Trust conservation areas and tours of other Trust properties are available.

Skagit Land Trust depends on the generosity of its supporters, members and friends. To become involved or to make a donation to protect Skagit lands, contact the Trust at:

SKAGIT LAND TRUST
Saving Land for Tomorrow

Skagit Land Trust
PO Box 1017
Mount Vernon, WA 98273
(360) 428-7878

Proceeds from the sale of this book go directly into conservation of wildlife habitat, forests, farms, shoreline, and open space in Skagit County, Washington.